VLADIMIR NABOKOV

Edited by Peter Quennell

His Life
His Work
His World

VLADIMIR NABOKOV

A tribute

Weidenfeld and Nicolson
London

Copyright material from the works of Vladimir Nabokov is reprinted by kind permission of the following (full publication details are given in the Bibliography): Mrs Vera Nabokov for material from *Speak, Memory*, copyright © 1960, 1966 by Vladimir Nabokov. New Directions Publishing Co. for material from *Real Life of Sebastian Knight*, copyright © 1941, 1959 by New Directions. G. P. Putnam's Sons for material from *The Defence*, copyright © 1964 by Vladimir Nabokov; from *Lolita*, copyright © 1955 by Vladimir Nabokov; from *The Gift*, copyright © 1963 by Vladimir Nabokov; from *Pale Fire*, copyright © 1962 by G. P. Putnam's Sons; from *Despair*, copyright © 1965, 1966 by Vladimir Nabokov. McGraw Hill Book Co. for material from *Transparent Things*, copyright © 1972 by Vladimir Nabokov; from *Ada*, copyright © 1969 by Vladimir Nabokov; from *King, Queen, Knave*, copyright © 1968 by Vladimir Nabokov. Doubleday & Co. Inc. and William Heinemann Ltd for material from *Pnin*, copyright © 1964 by Vladimir Nabokov. Bobbs-Merrill Co. Inc. and New Directions for material from *Laughter in the Dark*, copyright © 1938, 1960 by Vladimir Nabokov.

First published in Great Britain by
Weidenfeld & Nicolson Ltd
91 Clapham High Street, London SW4
1979

ISBN 0 297 77665 7

Set, printed and bound in Great Britain by
Fakenham Press Limited,
Fakenham, Norfolk

Contents

List of Illustrations

Introduction

Vladimir Nabokov entered the world in St Petersburg on 23 April 1899 and died, after more than half a century of exile, in Switzerland, at Montreux on 2 July 1977, where he had made his last home. He was the eldest son of a rich, highly cultivated and strongly liberal Russian family. During the early stages of the Revolution, his father, also named Vladimir, a leader of the progressive Cadet Party, took office under Kerensky's short-lived government; but, once the Bolsheviks had seized power, the Nabokov family left Russia, and moved first to London, then to Berlin, where the future novelist, having completed his education at Trinity College, Cambridge, rejoined them in 1922. Almost immediately he began his literary career; and between 1923 and 1940, using the Russian language, he published under the pseudonym 'Sirin' novels, short stories, plays, poems and translations – among them, a Russian version of *Alice in Wonderland* – that brought him considerable renown. In 1940 he crossed the Atlantic with his wife and son, and settled down to academic work, as a lecturer at Wellesley College from 1941 to 1948, and as Professor of Russian Literature at Cornell University from 1948 to 1959. *The Gift*, finished in 1937, was the last novel that he wrote in Russian; and it was followed in 1941 by *The Real Life of Sebastian Knight.* His literary merits were soon recognized; many editors appreciated his work, and were glad to print his stories; but not until the American edition of *Lolita* appeared in 1958 did he achieve resounding popular success.

Today Nabokov's fame is worldwide; and he is regarded as one of the most strikingly original novelists to emerge since Proust and Joyce – both of them, incidentally, writers for whom he had a deep respect. Not only did he gain a magnificent command of his second language, English, and develop an extraordinary narrative and descriptive skill, but he brought to his task a visionary insight, a romantic verve and a grasp of human character that seem peculiarly his own. He is always intensely himself, by turns tragic, comic, poetic, satirical, yet, at the same time, often warm and tender. In this volume a series of critics, both English and American, have combined to pay him homage; while his son and translator, Dmitri Nabokov, has contributed a delightful valediction that evokes his way of life, his methods of work and his endearing personal character. His wife and son, too, have provided hitherto unpublished photographs of the Nabokov household before 1917 and of Vyra, the estate near St Petersburg, so well described in *Speak, Memory*. From Nabokov's recollections of his supremely happy youth much of his adult inspiration sprang.

1 The Novelist's World

Peter Quennell

The shortest road to Montreux railway station from the Montreux Palace Hotel is a fairly prosaic stretch of urban pavement, overlooked by sombre concrete buildings; but Vladimir Nabokov, when he inhabited Montreux, made this journey almost every day, to purchase foreign newspapers at a bookstall near the station's lower entrance; and, I am told, he never found it dull. As he left the hotel, he recognized each of the trees he passed in the surrounding garden – their exact species, of course, he had long ago identified; for, besides being a well-known lepidopterist, he was a knowledgeable arboriculturalist and botanist; and his knowledge extended to the beasts and birds he had loved and studied since his boyhood. Though much of his adult life had been spent in large European cities and American university towns, he had remained on affectionate terms with Nature; and, asked by a transatlantic interviewer to describe how his working day began, he said that a yellow-billed Alpine chough, a 'big, glossy, black thing', which visited his balcony and emitted 'a most melodious chuckle', punctually aroused him at about seven o'clock.

In the range of his interests and his widespread curiosity Nabokov resembled a seventeenth-century polymath, an erudite yet discursive and imaginative author like Robert Burton or Sir Thomas Browne, rather than the average modern novelist. But his erudition and the use to which he put his researches form only a small part of his literary achievement. The novelist's function, I believe, is both to observe life and to produce his own universe, offering his readers (wrote Marcel Proust) 'a revelation of the world that we ourselves see and that our fellows cannot see. The pleasure the artist gives us depends on his ability to disclose a second universe beyond the one we know.'*

Such a revelation Nabokov, a great admirer of Proust's masterpiece, certainly accomplished in his novels and his stories; and here, while other contributors discuss the more specialized features of

* *Lettres de Marcel Proust à Bibesco*, edited by Thierry Maulnier, 1949.

his opus, I propose to examine some general characteristics of the Nabokovian world. Among its most remarkable features is its imaginative continuity; the reader feels that he is wandering around a landscape, where again and again he recognizes a vividly remembered detail – a river bank, a bridge, a summer-house, a forest path, a gloomy public garden, even a pane of coloured glass. That pane repeatedly turns up – I wonder if any student of Nabokov's work has yet counted its recurrences? – as do a host of complementary symbols. None is irrelevant; all belong to his past, to the romantic labyrinth of the *Temps perdu* through which he follows a fine golden thread. Proust could not recapture Combray; Nabokov could never hope to revisit the far-off Russian manor-house, now stolen and destroyed, at which he spent his happy youth. A sense of loss pervades his whole opus; but he escaped the ordinary exile's grudges, and the nostalgic emotions that haunted him were by no means deadening or self-destructive. They inspired him to create a new world, where every ancestral ghost could be laid, and the conflicting claims of past and present are mysteriously reconciled.

In a volume of tributes published before his death* Ross Wetzsteon provided an illuminating account of the novelist as a lecturer. His subject, at the time, was *Madame Bovary*; and he dwelt on Emma's eyes and hair, and said he would have liked to revise a contemporary English version, changing 'smooth' to 'sleek', 'curved' to 'dipped', and 'head' to 'skull'. It was the details he valued; 'caress the details,' he advised, 'the divine details!' Generalizations and general ideas, Mr Wetzsteon adds, 'were anathema to him – because he knew too much about the differences between things to generalize ... because, as he wrote ... the word "cosmic" is always in danger of losing its *s*'. The admirer of Flaubert and Proust was a lifelong lover of Chekhov; and *Strong Opinions*, a collection of reviews and critical notes, includes Nabokov's appraisal of an essay by Simon Karlinsky, 'Nabokov and Chekhov', printed in the same volume:

> He is right; I do love Chekhov dearly. ... I fail, however, to rationalize my feeling for him: I can easily do so in regard to the greater artist, Tolstoy, with the flash of this or that unforgettable passage ... but when I imagine Chekhov ... all I can make out is a medley of ... ready-made epithets, repetitions, doctors, unconvincing vamps ... yet it is *his* works that I would take on a trip to another planet.

* *Nabokov: Criticisms, reminiscences, translations and tributes*, edited by Alfred Appel, Jr and Charles Newman, 1970.

What fascinated Nabokov in Chekhov was evidently his use of detail – that and the enveloping atmosphere, about which Hannah Green, whose reminiscences we publish here, heard him speak at Wellesley College: 'Read and dream through Chekhov's bleak landscapes, which convey a dim loveliness and are like gray clothes on a gray clothesline flapping against a gray sky. . . . Chekhov's world is dove-gray.'

'The Ravine' and 'The Duel' were stories that he warmly recommended; but 'The Lady with the Dog' is a story that particularly reminds me of his method. Once Gurov has seduced his new conquest a sudden silence falls between them:

> The attitude of Anna Sergeyevna . . . to what had happened was somehow peculiar. . . . Her face drooped and faded, and on both sides of it her long hair hung down mournfully; she mused in a dejected attitude like 'the woman who was a sinner' in an old-fashioned picture. 'It's wrong', she said. 'You will be the first to despise me now.' There was a water-melon on the table. Gurov cut himself a slice and began eating it without haste.

Here the effect of emotional diminuendo that the writer wishes to convey and Gurov's gentle indifference (which a strong and lasting devotion will eventually replace) are subtly brought home by the fresh, clean taste of the slice of melon he enjoys, while his inexperienced mistress broods and mourns. Nabokov displays a similar aptitude for employing an expressive detail, whether it be comic or pathetic; and, when I read him, I often think of Proust's imaginary novelist Bergotte, who, during his later life, 'if he wished to speak well of a book, would always mention an incident that evoked an image. . . . "Ah, yes!", he would say, "that is good! There is a little girl wearing an orange shawl" . . . or again: "Oh yes! There is a passage where a regiment marches through a town. . . ."' Bergotte, too, distrusted generalizations and did his best to avoid the majestic truisms, the '*grands lieux communs*', that are apt to weigh down ideological literature. Like Nabokov, he would have firmly denied that he represented any school or had any social or political 'purpose', and would have agreed that art – again I quote from Simon Karlinsky – was 'not "about something" but the thing itself'; that 'literature does not tell the truth but makes it up'; and that, while 'great writers invent their own world', the less imaginative and creative storyteller merely embellishes established facts.

Nabokov's books are starred with passages that Bergotte would have immediately singled out, each a record of one of those rare revelatory moments around which a whole work of art may at length materialize. To distinguish and translate them into words he needed a marvellously perceptive eye; and a splendid example of how he fixed a scene and evoked a situation is provided by his masterly early novel *The Defence.* His chief character, a neurotic and backward child, has taken refuge, during his parents' musical party, in a dark, deserted room; and, as he hides there, the young violinist is called to a telephone that stands upon his father's table:

From time to time a faint glimmer sped over the ceiling in a mysterious arc and a gleaming dot showed on the desk – he did not know what; perhaps one facet of a paperweight in the guise of a heavy crystal egg or a reflection in the glass of a desk photograph. He had almost dozed off when suddenly he started at the ringing of a telephone on the desk ... The butler came in from the dining room, turned on in passing a light which illuminated only the desk, placed the receiver to his ear, and without noticing Luzhin went out again.... A minute later he returned accompanying a gentleman who ... picked up the receiver from the desk and with his other hand groped for the back of the desk chair. The servant closed the door behind him, cutting off the distant ripple of music. 'Hello,' said the gentleman.... 'No, I've already played', he said looking upwards, while his white restless hand fidgeted with something on the desk. A cab clip-clopped hollowly over the wooden pavement. 'I think so,' said the gentleman. Luzhin could see his profile – an ivory nose, black hair, a bushy eyebrow. 'Frankly, I don't know why you are calling me here,' he said quietly, continuing to fiddle with something on the desk. 'If it was only to check up ... You silly,' he laughed and commenced to swing one foot in its patent leather shoe regularly back and forth. Then he placed the receiver very skillfully between his ear and his shoulder and replying intermittently with 'yes' and 'no' and 'perhaps', used both hands to pick up the object he had been playing with on the desk....

I think also of an episode in *Speak, Memory*, his fascinating autobiographical excursion:

That summer I would always ride by a certain isba, golden in the low sun, in the doorway of which Polenka, the daughter of our head coachman Zahar, a girl of my age, would stand, leaning against the jamb, her bare arms folded on her breast in a soft, comfortable manner peculiar to rural Russia. She would watch me approach with a wonderful welcoming radiance on her face, but as I rode nearer, this would dwindle to a half smile, then to a faint light at the corners of her compressed lips, and, finally, this, too, would fade, so that when I reached her, there would be no expression at all on her round, pretty face. As soon as I had passed, however, and had turned my head for an instant to take a last look before sprinting uphill, the dimple would be back, the enigmatic light would be playing again on her dear features. I never spoke to her, but long after I had stopped riding by at that hour, our ocular relationship was renewed from time to time during two or three summers. She would appear from nowhere, always standing a little apart, always barefoot, rubbing her left instep against her right calf or scratching with her fourth finger the parting in her light brown hair, and always leaning against things....

I have transcribed these long extracts for several different reasons. Not only do they show Nabokov's gift of evoking an atmosphere and, by a delicately suggestive choice of details, establishing its proper background; but they emphasize the odd resemblance (which has sometimes occurred to me) between Nabokov and Laurence Sterne, a novelist he much esteemed. Both writers have an extravagant sense of humour and a wild erotic fancy; and both depict their characters' movements, expressions and gestures with meticulous exactitude. For Sterne, I have suggested elsewhere, 'appearances were as essential an expression of personality as the mind or soul itself; the inward and outward were part of the same fabric.... Truth was revealed on the surface, as well as underneath the surface. And it is with the surface Sterne begins....' Nabokov's picture of the young violinist talking impatiently to his tiresome female caller, and his portrait of Polenka, with her vague erotic charm and meaningful, yet ultimately meaningless smile, would have gone straight to Yorick's heart.

There the resemblance ceases. Nabokov had as keen a vision as Sterne; but his emotional scope was far wider. So is the range of his imagery – a subject that has not yet received all the attention it deserves from English and American critics. Every distinguished writer has certain images he especially delights in; and Nabokov had a particular affection for images of shade and sunshine. I doubt if any novelist, new or old, has been more attached to shadows and their exquisite gradations. Thus, *Mary*, his first novel, published in 1926, contains a memorable account of a romantic sea voyage:

Then came several glorious, sad days at sea. Like two floating white wings the oncoming foam embraced everything, embraced the bow of the steamer ... and the green shadows of people leaning on the ship's rails flickered softly across the bright slopes of the waves.... Two seagulls glided round the funnel and their wet bills, caught in a ray of sunshine, flashed like diamonds.

I have noted many other passages of the same kind – in *The Defence* (1930), where 'reflected gleams of whitish light unfolded fanwise, bringing [Luzhin's] face to light, and the soft shadow made by his nose circled slowly over his cheek and then his lip, and again it was dark until another light went by ...'; and in 'The Vane Sisters' (1959), an evocative long short story, where the narrator pauses as he walks about the town, to observe 'a family of brilliant icicles drip-dripping from the eaves of a frame house. So clear-cut were their pointed shadows ... that I was sure the shadows of the falling drops should be visible too.' He is disappointed, until he reaches another house and, looking up at the eaves of the garage 'with its full display of transparent stalactites backed by their blue silhouettes', watches, on choosing a silhouette, 'what might be described as the dot of an exclamation mark leaving its ordinary position to glide down very fast – a jot faster than the thaw-drop it raced'.

Though often elusive and poetic, at times Nabokov's images are almost brutally precise, witness his portrait of Sybil, the younger Vane girl, condemned to a miserable early death:

> During one hundred and fifty minutes my gaze kept reverting to her ... and kept observing that carefully waved dark hair, that small, small flowered hat with a little hyaline veil ... and under it her small face broken into a cubist pattern by scars due to a skin disease, pathetically masked by a sun-lamp tan that had hardened her features whose charm was further impaired by her having painted everything that could be painted, so that the pale gums of her teeth between cherry-red chapped lips and the darkened blue ink of her eyes under darkened lids were the only visible openings into her beauty.

In an anthology planned to illustrate Nabokov's descriptive powers, passages that deal with solid but inanimate objects would deserve a lengthy section. I can think of no novelist, writing at the present time, who gives such objects a more vital shape; and his attitude towards them frequently reminds one of Nerval's mysterious sonnet 'Vers dorés', which celebrates a pantheistic universe where everything, flowers, metal, stones, possesses its own secret life – '*ce monde où la vie éclate en toute chose*' – and even the blank wall may conceal an eye that is covertly regarding us. For Nabokov, chairs and looking-glasses play a large part in the human comedy. The wicker armchair, 'out of sheer fright, bursts into a salvo of crackling' when an obese French governess cautiously prepares to sit down; and the glass, 'hanging on taut cords, its pure brow inclined ... strives to retain the falling furniture and the slope of bright floor that keep slipping from its embrace'. Nabokov's trains and railway carriages – he mentions the lingering sigh with which a carriage halts – are no less strongly individual. He had adored the luxurious *wagon-lits* that, during his childhood, had carried his cosmopolitan family across Europe; and both trains themselves and the curious landscapes of stations and railway-tracks always excited his imagination:

A cloud of locomotive steam [we read in *The Gift*] suddenly appeared from the right of the bridge, disintegrated against its iron ribs, then immediately loomed white again on the other side and wavily streamed away.... Crossing the bridge ... Fyodor, as usual, was gladdened by the wonderful poetry of railroad banks, by their free and diversified nature: a growth of locusts and sallows, wild grass, bees, butterflies – all this lived in isolation and unconcern in the harsh vicinity of coal dust ... and in blissful estrangement from the city coulisses above, from the peeled walls of old houses toasting their tattooed backs in the morning sunshine.

The glimpse of old houses warming their tattooed backs is a peculiarly Nabokovian image; but I suspect I may have already written enough about the novelist's descriptive genius, and possibly given the impression that what I most admire in his work is the mosaic of 'divine details'. This would be misleading; though I appreciate his details for their own sake, I also value them because they are so closely allied to the general framework of his universe. He had a marvellously receptive mind. His friends, Alfred Appel records, were at once 'impressed by his intense and immense curiosity, his uninhibited and imaginative response to everything around him.' To paraphrase Henry James's famous definition, 'Nabokov [was] truly a man on whom nothing is lost'; and, unlike James, he never overlooked 'the sometimes extraordinarily uncommon qualities of the commonplace'. He relished and respected life; *Lolita* itself, despite the picture it draws of a doomed perversion, becomes at last a hymn in praise of love. The vulgar yet seductive little girl poor Humbert had desired beyond endurance has lost, when he meets her for the last time, every trace of childish beauty:

Couple of inches taller. Pink-rimmed glasses. New, heaped-up hairdo, new ears.... She was frankly and hugely pregnant. Her head looked smaller (only two seconds had passed really, but let me give them as much wooden duration as life can stand), and her pale freckled arms were hollowed, and her bare shins and arms had lost all their tan, so that the little hairs showed. She wore a brown, sleeveless cotton dress and sloppy felt slippers.

Yet, at this moment, a miraculous transformation overtakes his heart and senses:

What I used to pamper among the tangled vines of my heart, *mon grand péché radieux*, had dwindled to its essence: sterile and selfish vice, all *that* I cancelled and cursed. . . . I insist the world know how much I loved my Lolita, pale and polluted, and big with another's child, but still grey-eyed, still sooty-lashed . . . still Carmencita, still mine. . . .

Amid the hubbub of applause and abuse that greeted the appearance of *Lolita*, Lionel Trilling's pronouncement was the most decisive: 'Lolita is about love. . . . In recent fiction no lover has thought of his beloved with so much tenderness . . . it is one of the few examples of rapture in modern writing.' The passage that I have just quoted contains learned references both to Verlaine on the subject of his beloved Rimbaud and to Catullus on his faithless Lesbia; and only Nabokov, I think, would have made such apposite yet unobtrusive use of them. In Nabokov's world Love, under all its different guises, from rapturous physical passion to calm aesthetic delight, is always the creative spirit. True, the passions and affections he describes may be the products of a wild illusion and his amorists cloud-pursuing centaurs; but then, illusion, too, is an aspect of human existence; and Humbert Humbert, at the tragic end of his career, does not feel that his pursuit was wasted.

In the last paragraph of *Lolita* – the novel that I myself think was unquestionably his masterpiece, since it combines almost all the attributes of his earlier and later books, poetic, elegiac, romantic, satiric, fantastic and grotesque – Humbert promises his beloved immortality: 'while the blood still throbs through my writing hand, you are still as much part of blessed matter as I am'. In 'the refuge of art' she has an unalterable place; 'this is the only immortality you and I may share, my Lolita'. Art alone can give an illusion substance, and disclose its hidden value; and Humbert, so long a frustrated artist, suddenly sees light ahead. The personal fulfilment he could not achieve on earth may still be reached in the secondary world of recollection and imagination. Like Proust's Narrator, who is also nearing his end, he watches all the chaotic experiences of his previous life fall at last into a comprehensive pattern.

2 Remembering Nabokov

Alfred Appel Jnr

I am thinking of aurochs and angels, the secret of durable pigments, prophetic sonnets, the refuge of art. And this is the only immortality you and I may share, my Lolita.

Vladimir Nabokov, *Lolita*

In *Finnegans Wake*, Joyce writes, 'It darkels ... all this our funnaminal world.' This isn't very tough-going for the *Wake*: 'darkels' = dark + sparkles; 'funnaminal' = phenomenal + fundamental + fun animal. The *'sublime Dublinois'*, Humbert Humbert calls Joyce, and though wordsmith Nabokov favoured verbal effects and games more openly grounded and mobile than those of *Finnegans Wake* (the finest car in *Ada* is a 'Jolls-Joyce'), he might have created that pun-cluster from the *Wake* as part of a valedictory statement quite uniquely his. Was Kafka a 'fun animal', as it were? Proust certainly was not, enclosed in his cork-lined room. But Vladimir Nabokov was, pre-eminently; and I am going to remember my teacher and friend as he lived – a great and most resilient celebrant of life. My remarks, then, will be for the most part in the Irish spirit of a wake. And, if by 'Irish' we mean an open and unfettered enjoyment of the world, Vladimir Nabokov was more Irish than James Joyce, whose *Ulysses* Nabokov revered more than any novel except *Anna Karenina.* These two novels, along with Kafka's 'The Metamorphosis' and Proust's *Swann's Way*, were always the highlights of Nabokov's annual spring lecture course, to which I will now turn.

The scene: well-worn and spacious lecture room B, Goldwin Smith Hall, Cornell University, May 1954, a room whose excellent lighting encouraged co-eds to over-indulge a romantic but aurally annoying campus fad of the fifties: knitting in class (socks or scarf for a steady boyfriend, the needles clicking and tapping *I love you*). Professor V. Nabokov is lecturing to some two hundred undergraduates in Literature 312, his 'Masterpieces of European Fiction' course. It is unseasonably warm this particular noon; a torpor has settled over the students; there seems to be a mist rising from fraternity row, the sea of

C-minuses at the rear of the room. Hardly a needle stirs in the house. That steady yet gentle static, or morse code, is absent for once. Professor Nabokov pauses between sentences and then, as if startled by the touch of some invisible hand, looks up from his notes and, in a voice far more intimate than that of our casually formal thespian-lecturer, asks, 'Did you hear that? A cicada is singing, perhaps in this room.' Suddenly Professor Nabokov has our attention, the sort paid to any harmless fellow when he is about to formulate his madness. 'Yes, a cicada. I think it is on that window sill,' he says, pointing to the right. 'Please check it for us,' he asks a young man slumped by the window, who struggles to his white-bucked feet as if roused from a dream. 'It's *two* grasshoppers,' the student reports, an unwitting straight man for Professor Nabokov, who, playing Groucho Marx to the student's Chico, now lowers his head, peers over his glasses, wide-eyed, and corrugates his brow – a characteristic expression – as if to ask, wordlessly, that painful question: *Cicadus interruptus*? The class laughs, a breeze stirs. *Homo ludens*, to pin down Nabokov with the proper Latin nomenclature, as befits a distinguished lepidopterist. Man playing, but not frivolously.

'Do you know *how* the cicada makes its music and *why*?' asks Professor Nabokov, who discerns the collective answer quickly enough, without a show of hands or a secret ballot. He draws the insect on the blackboard; then he explains, and his voice rises in excitement and he stammers as he extends the digression, adding lore about the cicada and information about its appearances in art – the mosaics of Pompeii! – and literature; an updated provenance would today include line 182 of the poem *Pale Fire*, where 'the cicada sings' for John Shade's sixty-first birthday. The student seated to my left is taking notes, furiously. His neighbour on the other side leans over and hisses, 'Hey schmoe, whadya doin'? This isn't going to be on the final!' 'But it's so interesting, so interesting,' answers the note-taker. Nabokov concludes and returns to Joyce. The mists have cleared, needles whirr and click, and our attention is once again fixed on the details – always the details – of the text under precise taxonomic scrutiny; *Details of a Sunset* (1976) would be the title of his final book. Detail and precision: the cornerstones of any genuine scholarship, obviously, and certainly of Nabokov's greatness as a writer. 'I have never known anyone more learned in the literal sense of the term than Vladimir; the quantity, the precision, the depth of his knowledge was an astonishment and a delight,' states Arthur Mizener, the biographer of F. Scott Fitzgerald, Nabokov's friend and colleague for almost a decade, from 1951 to 1959 (see his fine tribute in *Cornell Alumni News*, September 1977). 'Do you know the name of that tree?' Professor Nabokov asked one of my friends, an aspiring undergraduate author who had come to Nabokov's office for some professional tips. 'No,' he replied, after politely glancing out of the window in the general direction of Nabokov's gesture. 'Then you'll never be a writer,' said Nabokov.

'As a writer, I am half-painter, half-naturalist,' Nabokov wrote to me in 1966; and the desk in his study, observed by this potential Kinbote later in the year, represented that combination and equipoise most elegantly. Arranged along the desk-top were a framed butterfly; a small dark family photograph (*c.* 1905), shadows of the past sanctified in *Speak, Memory*; and a postcard reproduction of the serene and symmetrical *Annunciation* by Fra Angelico (*c.* 1450) in which the angel Gabriel has the rainbow wings of a butterfly or tropical bird – 'rather pavonian', Nabokov might have called them, and I presume, now, with one of those 'dictionary' words which suggest to some that his vocabulary could be too fancy, or that ours is too limited and wanting in precision. Standing at his portable lectern, seated at that nearby desk, or lying on the bed (gravity versus the artist), Nabokov laboured over each sentence, on one of his famous 3″ × 5″ index cards, as though he were a medieval or Renaissance miniaturist rather than a nineteenth-century muralist (he himself always favoured visual and painterly metaphors when describing his work, his intentions and his procedures). Did Professor Nabokov say that the cicada was best rendered by Dürer? I cannot recall; I did not take notes; *I* am no schmoe. But I did remember those seven or so digressive minutes a few years later when I read the following in 'Time and Ebb', Nabokov's story of 1945: 'Attainment and science, retainment and art – the two couples keep to themselves, but when they do meet, nothing else in the world matters.' Chapter 6 of *Speak, Memory*, the butterfly chapter, is as joyful as any of several such meetings, or couplings, in his work; and one parenthetical reference to the young lepidopterist's guiding angel, 'whose wings, except for the absence of a Florentine limbus, resemble those of Fra Angelico's Gabriel' – an addition to the 1966 text – suggests that the vivid postcard on his desk-top was suggestive enough. 'My guiding angel [continues the passage in question] pointed out to me a rare visitor [on the honeysuckle], a splendid, pale-yellow creature with black blotches, blue crenels, and a cinnabar eyespot above each chrome-rimmed black tail.' Highlighted by a small but amusing surprise (the automotive or Art Deco chrome), the passage is typical of the cooler procedures of half-naturalist Nabokov, and, save for the blue, perfectly drawn or painted.

'Before the advent of Pushkin and Gogol, European literature was blind,' declared Professor Nabokov in his initial lecture on *Dead Souls*, autumn 1953. 'It saw colour in the hackneyed terms of the ancients: the sky was blue, the dawn red, the foliage green, and the clouds grey, which is meaningless, of course.' Nabokov's own palette – 'pal-ette, "little friend", good name for it,' he might well have said – his palette as a writer was subtly variegated. In *Speak, Memory*, for instance, he offers 'blue-white' (the optical phenomenon of shadows on bright snow), 'misty-blue', 'purplish-blue', 'silvery blue', 'cobalt blue', 'indigo blue', 'azure', 'china-blue', 'dove-blue', 'crystal blue', 'ice-bright' (water) – but never, no, certainly not, *never* – well, *almost* never – imprecise, jejune, plain *blue*! – if I may offer a taxonomy in the manner of our subject. And the colour that some of us would recognize, record and accept as 'brown', is transcribed by Nabokov as no less than thirteen different tints and combinations, though it is probably too soon for another *catalogue raisonné* of colours. In *Ada* (1969), half-painter Nabokov writes, 'Remembrance, like Rembrandt, is dark and festive.' Multicoloured or monochromatic, Nabokov's visual prose emits a glow that is old-fashioned in more than one way, as I shall shortly suggest.

'My task which I am trying to achieve is . . . before all, to make you *see*. That – and no more, and it is everything,' stated Joseph Conrad in his famous preface to *The Negro of the 'Narcissus'*. Nabokov, who early on titled a novella *The Eye* (1930), could do this with a sensuous specificity as exact as any writer of the century, whether he was describing a curds-and-whey cloud formation, a clear and lambent sky, the details of a sunset (see the last paragraph, Chapter 10, *Speak, Memory*). Yet his landscapes are not isolated set pieces, mere 'pretty pictures'; and a brief and slyly involuted passage in *Transparent Things* (1972) serves to remind us that there is often more than greets the eye in such writing. 'Using ink and aquarelle I can paint a lake-scape of unsurpassed translucence with all the mountains of paradise reflected therein,' Hugh Person writes in his diary, 'but am unable to draw . . . the silhouette of human panic in the blazing windows of a villa'; which in fact prefigures the final passage of Hugh Person and

Transparent Things, and keynotes too their maker's life-long preoccupation with death, his ability 'to draw' and sometimes ease our shared or collective eschatological panic. Note too the penultimate page of *Lolita*, when Humbert looks into the 'friendly abyss' where visual beauty and moral truth are perceived simultaneously, an ideal union. All this is basically quite amazing, of course: a cosmopolitan modern writer, who even in his darkest works manages to salute, however fleetingly, the sparkling wonders of the natural world. Of all things! Compare Nabokov with the implosive Samuel Beckett, say ('There's no more nature' [*Endgame*]), or with Borges, whose quotidian is the library. Nabokov was bookish, too; and he esteemed the prose music of Beckett's *Molloy*; but the geography of that extraordinary and most hopeful of Beckett's works, with its place-names of 'Bally', 'Hole' and, far lower on the map, 'Turdy', serves to underscore further the singular radiance of Nabokov's phenomenal findings. 'Weeds and fungi, and ridgelike tree roots crossed and recrossed the sun-flecked trails,' writes Nabokov in Chapter 6 of *Speak, Memory*, describing how the flora had defied and eluded the strict gardeners at the summer estate of his Russian boyhood. 'On a picturesque boulder, a little mountain ash and a still smaller aspen had climbed, holding hands, like two clumsy, shy children.' For an example of a contemporary sensibility akin to this aspect of Nabokov's (if examples are instructive), one must turn to another medium, and the silver prints of photographer Ansel Adams (b. 1902). 'A great artist!' exclaimed Nabokov in 1974, when I showed him several reproductions of Adams's most lyrical landscapes.

The naturalist's acute eye served the bemused émigré well while he was slowly discovering, gathering and inventing American *couleur locale* (as Humbert might call it) for *Lolita*, observing, observing wherever he went. Professor Robert Martin Adams, then in the English department at Cornell ('Ah, a duel!' Nabokov had exclaimed, when Adams appeared at the departmental office one morning with his newly broken arm in a sling), remembers a Monday morning in June in about 1951, during the calm between commencement and summer session. A convocation of a youth group was to begin that day – the Young Lutherans or Future Farmers of America; and, as Adams approached the wide bridge that separates the campus from the main dormitory area, he saw heading towards him, on the left side of the bridge, radiating the healthiness of a breakfast-food advertisement, a seemingly endless swarm of blond and apple-cheeked junior and senior high-schoolers; and, on the other side, walking alone in the opposite direction, his steady gaze recording and storing them on cranial snapshots, a husky middle-aged man wearing hiking shoes, knee socks, baggy Bermuda shorts, a sporty cap, and carrying a butterfly net. As it crossed the bridge, the Norman Rockwell *tableau vivant* turned as one to stare in astonishment at *him*, since Nabokov was no doubt the first typical American college professor they had ever seen. They understood what a more sophisticated audience would subsequently grant: admire it or not, the art of Nabokov is *sui generis*.

One may see Nabokov's eye in action, quite literally, in the late Robert Hughes's excellent 1965 National Educational Television film about him. In one scene we follow Nabokov as he walks through Montreux. Traffic. A news kiosk. A woman making a call inside a lone glass *moderne* telephone booth, her dog waiting impatiently outside. When Nabokov sees the phone booth, he stops, and, biting his lower lip, quickly jots down something in a little notebook – or has he made a sketch? – the surprising intensity of his sudden concentration moving the film viewer to look more carefully at the mundane locus before us. The dog's leash, a taut diagonal extending into the booth, now comes into focus; and the scene is transformed: a dog taking a booth for a walk? Or a booth taking a dog for a walk? One suddenly saw too why Nabokov and Saul Steinberg admired each other's work so much. But what *did* Nabokov write in his notebook? Perhaps his inspired entry was merely a reminder to buy more index cards, aspirin and soap; or, worse, it was a meaningless squiggle performed by thespian Nabokov for the eye of the dumb camera – to reassert the spirit of the wake by deflating my (strabismic?) speculations in a manner that duplicates or approaches the way Nabokov often toyed with his audience.

As a lecturer, Nabokov was on occasion an excellent actor, making full use of his expressive face and rich, accented baritone voice. Certain performances remain firmly in one's mind. The setting is again Goldwin Smith B, November 1953. With Christmas gifts perhaps on their minds, the co-ed artisans seem to be embarked on uncommonly ambitious projects, long woollen items in Cornell red and Dartmouth green (winter underwear? one-piece snowsuits?), knitting them with the doggedness of so many Madame Defarges at an execution. Professor Nabokov is lamenting Gogol's religious conversion, the artistic lameness of the unfinished second volume of *Dead*

Souls, and Gogol's decline and horrendous slide, the knitting needles all the while sounding their customary descant: click clack, click clack, click clack. Then Nabokov rehearses Gogol's death agonies: how the hack doctors alternately bled him and purged him and plunged him into icy baths (click clack, click clack); Gogol so frail that his spine could be felt through his stomach, the six fat white bloodletting leeches clinging to his nose (click clack); Gogol begging to have them removed – 'Please lift them, lift them, keep them away!' Sinking behind the lectern, now a tub (click), Nabokov for several moments *was* Gogol, shuddering and shivering, his hands held down by a husky attendant, his head thrown back in pain and terror, nostrils distended, eyes shut, his beseechments filling the large and hushed lecture hall. The most ambitious of note-takers are motionless, red and green woollen tentacles hang limply from co-ed laps. Even the sea of C-minuses in the back of the room cannot help being moved. (Today, twenty-five years later, as I replay the scene and Nabokov holds that pose, a silhouette of human panic, eyes closed, I am reminded of David's famous painting, *Marat Assassinated* (1793), alluded to in *Lolita* and *Pale Fire*.) Then, after a pause, Nabokov would say, dispassionately, in a sentence drawn word for word from his *Nikolai Gogol* (1944), 'Although the scene is unpleasant and has a human appeal which I deplore, it is necessary to dwell upon it a little longer in order to bring out the curiously physical side of Gogol's genius.' The rhetoric of Nabokov's fiction manipulates readers in an analogous fashion, as in the following short passage, typical of the thousand-and-one (or so) tonal trapdoors in *Lolita*, this one sprung neatly in the restful space between the two sentences. Naked, shaking with fever, Lolita 'complained of a painful stiffness in the upper vertebrae – and I thought of poliomyelitis as any American parent would. Giving up all hope of intercourse, I wrapped her up in a laprobe and carried her into the car.'

The Death of Gogol was a set piece, an annual performance. Although Nabokov's Cornell lectures had been fully written-out by hand and then typed by Véra Nabokov, he still took pride, as late as 1974, in the possibility that 'no one knew I was reading my lectures'. Actually he would sometimes call attention to this fact in class by making an unremarkable comment, then stopping to jot it down quickly, chuckling with delight – an 'ad lib'! – whether the addition to the script was a small joke or a serious observation. Along with instances of enthusiastic digressions (the cicada), he was capable of the most dramatic kind of spontaneous improvisations. Witness a noon lecture, February 1953, a semester before I took the two-part course. It was a cold day, cloudless and silver-skied, the clean hard snow and icicles around Goldwin Smith Hall glinting in the sun. Professor Nabokov, however, was quite dull as he asserted the greatness of *Anna Karenina* in an abstract manner uncharacteristic of him. Despite his exquisite diction and the almost musical way he enunciated and caressed her name – '*AHH*-nuh,' his voice falling and fading with the second syllable – Professor Nabokov was, as they say in show business, losing the audience, bombing in Ithaca, and the vulgarity of that phrase is equal to our capacity, our *genius* for distraction and boredom. Determine the size of each icicle family outside every window, see which window wins, *then* count the number of seconds between successive dripdrops of melting ice and compute the average time-lapse between drips.

Nabokov stopped lecturing, abruptly, and, without a word, strode to the right-hand side of the stage and snapped off the three overhead light fixtures. Then he walked down the five or six steps to the floor of the lecture hall, clumped up the aisle to the back, two hundred dismayed heads turning together – the Young Lutherans again – to watch him as he silently pulled down the shades of three or four large windows, curtaining those dazzling icicles and darkening the room (the other window shades were already drawn, thanks to an Art History slide show in the previous class). Nabokov retreated down the aisle, up the stairs, and returned to stage right and the control switch. 'In the firmament of Russian literature,' he proclaimed, 'this is Pushkin!' The ceiling light on the far left of the planetarium went on. 'This is Gogol!' The middle light went on. 'This is Chekhov!' The light on the right went on. Then Nabokov descended the stage once again, marched to the rear and the central window, and released the window shade, which sprang back on its roller (bang!), a solid wide beam of brilliant sunlight streaming into the room, like some emanation. 'And that is Tolstoy!' boomed Nabokov. Let it be said, however anticlimatically, that the class was convinced, its sense of Tolstoy's greatness predicated on a dead writer's ability to fire the imagination of a professor. Only now do I recognize the risk he took – what if clouds had suddenly covered the sun? – and, to employ once again the kind of painterly analogies he favoured, recognize, too, how much the Mannerist lighting effect owed to one of God's competitors in this area: Caravaggio or Rembrandt or La Tour.

Professor Nabokov used the blackboard with a flourish, too. For his initial lecture on 'The Metamorphosis' he would cover the 'grayboard' (as Professor Nominalist preferred to call it) with two huge drawings of Gregor Samsa – one a profile view, the other as seen from above, each at least 4′ × 2′, or 4″ × 2″ if you were seated on fraternity row; and then, since there is no sustained description of Gregor in the narrative, Nabokov proceeded to enumerate some fourteen entomological characteristics and mannerisms of Gregor, that, distributed through the text, serve to define him as a scarab or dung beetle – 'a bug among humbug', Nabokov would say, referring to Gregor's dreadful family. Next, Nabokov would explain the transformation in starkly fundamental human terms, asking us to imagine Gregor's spectral existence as a salesman, the unreality of all those hotel rooms in strange towns: 'Where am I? [Gregor, awakened by a nightmare, sitting up in an unfamiliar bed.] Who am I? *What* am I?' wondered the émigré, veteran of an infinite regress of rented rooms. A metamorphosis seemed to be an inevitable phenomenon; check your foot, yearn for a mirror. But at the outset of the following lecture, it was once again Entomology 312. 'This arrived in the mail this morning,' announced Nabokov; and, holding a thin beetle-brown volume as far away from his torso as his arm extension would allow – as though it were a vermin-infested, contaminated or radioactive object – he read aloud from what he described as 'an elegant and expensive new *illustrated* [he shudders] edition', whose translator had substituted 'cockroach' for 'gigantic insect' in the famous opening sentence. '*Cockroach!*' Nabokov repeated, assuming the expression of a person who had consumed rancid pizza with a chaser of warm sour goat's milk. 'Even the Samsa maid knows enough to call Gregor a dung beetle!' As for the illustrations, 'They don't even *resemble* Gregor.'

The Cockroach Fallacy, rampant in Kafka scholarship, continued to bug Nabokov, as he might pun, but only to demonstrate his command of *Amerikanski* slang, though he might pull his head back to slip the phantom blow warranted by such a verbal misdemeanour. Two decades later, in Montreux, the subject of Gregor's species and genus came up again, predictably; but then Nabokov surprised me. 'You know, I used to ride on the Berlin Elevated [train] with Kafka, in 1922 or '23 [he names the specific railway line] – 1923? yes, autumn '23 – in the early evening, when I was returning to my room. Often he sat across from me. Of course, I didn't know it then, but I am certain it was Kafka [who died in 1924]. One could not forget that face, its pallor, the tightness of the skin, those most extraordinary eyes, hypnotic eyes glowing in a cave. [The last phrase is very close to what John Ray, Jr, says of Humbert's narrative 'mask' in *Lolita*'s mock Foreword.] Years later when I first saw a photo of Kafka I recognized him immediately. And more recently I learned from [Max Brod's] biography, or Kafka's letters, that he and his mistress lived in the district where that man departed each time [he names the train stop]. He was on his way to see his mistress! [Pause. An attempt to picture Kafka and his Dora at home, happy? Impossible prospect!] Imagine: I could have spoken to Kafka! But what would I have said?' Nabokov added, with genuine alarm, as though the opportunity were real. ('So why join in the vulgar laughter? Why/scorn a hereafter none can verify:/The Turk's delight, the future lyres, the talks/With Socrates and Proust in cypress walks,' writes John Shade in his poem, *Pale Fire*). '*Ah!* [Nabokov's face brightens] I could remind Kafka that Gregor was a scarab beetle with wing-sheaths, for neither Gregor nor his maker realized that when the room was being made by the maid, and the window was open, he could have flown out and escaped and joined the other happy dung beetles rolling their dung balls on rural paths.' Later in the evening, Nabokov returned to the subject (a teacher's job is never done). 'By the way, do you know how a dung beetle lays its eggs?' he asked me. No, I answered, probably not as well as I should. Thespian-entomologist Nabokov imitated the process as best he could, bending his head towards his waist as he slowly walked across the living-room, making a dung-rolling motion with his hands until his head was buried in them and the eggs were laid.

Several other memories of Nabokov preserve for me the abundant fun he found or made for himself and others, not to mention his readers. Once, most likely during the winter of 1954, I sat behind the Nabokovs at an Ithaca movie theatre. The picture was *Beat the Devil*, the bizarrely humorous Truman Capote-John Huston shaggy-dog thriller. Nabokov was so amused that his loud laughter became conspicuous immediately. Véra Nabokov murmured '*Volodya!*' a few times, but then gave up, as it became clear that two comic fields of force had been established in the theatre: those who were laughing at the movie, and those who were laughing at (nameless) Nabokov laughing at the movie. At one juncture in the film, actor Peter Lorre approaches an artist who is painting a portrait of a man. Lorre studies the picture, a profile view, and then complains, in his famous nasal whine, 'That doesn't look like him. It has only one ear!' Nabokov exploded – that is the only verb – with laughter. It seemed to lift him from his seat, 'higher and higher, like old ... Nijinski, like Old Faithful' – I exaggerate, of course, but I'm quoting from the description in *Lolita* of Quilty's response to Humbert's initially harmless yet stimulating bullets, because I like to think that this great comic passage, written in the winter or spring of 1954, was inspired by the elixir of Nabokov's own laughter in the dark, to borrow his resonant title.

'To borrow and to borrow and to borrow ... as the Bard said, with that cold in his head,' hack writer Quilty tells Humbert, who has tracked him down to his baroque Pavor [Latin: 'fear'] Manor, where he kills Quilty for his abuses of language as well as for his misuse of Lolita. Nabokov in conversation toyed with language continuously; and, though he worked slowly and carefully on his prose, his written puns must have come to him quickly and easily. Two examples: when my wife and I visited Montreux in 1970 Nabokov was most interested to know if my classes at Northwestern University had been disrupted by demonstrations. No, nothing very dramatic, I replied, apart from one male student who expressed his disapproval of the war in Vietnam by calling me a eunuch. 'Oh, no, Alfred, you misunderstood him,' Nabokov said quickly. 'He called you "a unique".' 'My classroom problems are not political,' I continued. I told him about a nun who sat in the back row of one of my lecture courses, and who one day complained after class that a couple near her were always spooning. 'Sister,' I had said, 'in these troubled times we should be grateful if that's all they were doing'; and I related this to Nabokov rather smugly, proud of what I deemed to be my quick wit. 'Ohhh,' moaned Nabokov, mourning my lost opportunity, clapping his hand to his head in mock anguish. 'You should have said, "Sister, be grateful that they were not forking."'

The brilliance of at least the latter pun reinforces one's sense of that aura of invincibility and absolute authority which Nabokov projected so successfully in his many prefaces, interviews and letters to the editor (see his *Strong Opinions*, 1973). Yet the protective coloration of that persona (personae?), characterized by some as 'cold', 'arrogant', or 'imperial', is in a way unfortunate, inasmuch as it allowed no hint of the gentleness and sweetness that Nabokov, ensconced in Montreux, extended to casual visitors, friends, and, of course, to his family. Sympathetic readers of Nabokov should not find this surprising, given the authenticity of the filial love and tenderness expressed in so many of his works: *The Gift* (1938), *Speak, Memory*, and *Pale Fire* (1962), where John Shade observes that his homely and gentle daughter, Hazel, subsequently a suicide, had been cast in the school play not as a fairy or elf but 'as Mother Time,/A bent charwoman with slop pail and broom,/And like a fool I sobbed in the men's room'. Or the awkward overtures made by Pnin (1957) to his surrogate son, Victor (the gift of a football to an unathletic boy); the anguish of widower Adam Krug in *Bend Sinister* (1947), when he learns that his young son has been murdered by the State; the anxieties of the Russian widow who has not been told yet that her son has died in 'Breaking the News' (1935), the émigré precursor of 'Signs and Symbols' (1948), whose desperately hopeful parents refuse to read the deathly coded messages alluded to in the story's title; or the grief of the father for his dead son in 'Christmas' (1924), a very early tale arrayed in that concluding volume, *Details of a Sunset.*

How fitting that Nabokov, whose love for his father shines from so many pages, should have as *his* principal translator his own son, Dmitri (nine books in English, *Transparent Things* into Italian). And 'translation' may well be the central metaphor for what happens in every act of human speech, in every (imperfect?) attempt to communicate and interpret the word and the world. The fantastic verbal games of *Pale Fire* certainly suggest as much, as did Nabokov's almost fanatical devotion to his theory and practice of absolutely literal and utilitarian verse translation, 'beauty' sacrificed to accuracy, his only formal religious belief. By the time the novel's title passage from *Timon of Athens* (Act IV, Scene 3) has been translated from English to Zemblan and reversed into English again, the sun and the moon have exchanged genders, Shakespeare's phrase 'pale fire' has disappeared altogether, and we are indeed in the dark ('I live like Timon in his cave,' says Kinbote), asked to confront and contemplate the mysteries of identity and communication and perception. The brilliant fun – pointless or off-putting to lazy, complacent readers – here adumbrates fundamental concerns.

Because of the intensity of his love for his wife and his father, whose liberal ideals he shared, the author of *Pale Fire* could himself translate experience poorly. As jurist, editor and journalist, V. D. Nabokov was a notably active foe of anti-Semitism. It was nevertheless unusual for someone in his 'set' to marry a Jewish woman, as his son did in

Germany in 1925. Young Nabokov was thus at least doubly sensitive to the perniciousness of anti-Semitism. He would tolerate neither insults nor the blandest of innuendoes. Subtle protests are scattered throughout his American works. The class list of forty names at Lo's school, an American archetype memorized by Humbert and interpolated in his text, includes 'Flashman, Irving'. Humbert offers brief comments on several of the children, concluding with 'Irving, for whom I am sorry.' Why is he sorry for him? 'Poor Irving,' answered Nabokov, 'he is the only Jew among all those Gentiles.' Doubtless Nabokov's detestation of Ezra Pound – 'that total fake' – was based on the poet's fascist and anti-Semitic opinions, as well as on the artistic clutter and confusion of his *Cantos.* The subject of poor Ezra (as he was deemed by many intellectuals) came up for discussion in about 1954 at an Ithaca cocktail party given by the Nabokovs in the house they were renting that semester. Professor Arthur Mizener was at the centre of a group, telling them about another party, this one given by the poet Delmore Schwartz during the summer of 1950, in Gambier, Ohio, while the annual Kenyon School of Letters was convening. Schwartz's guests were discussing the continuing controversy surrounding the awarding of the Bollingen Prize to Pound, an Axis collaborator. Schwartz, who had consumed a fair share of his own liquor, began to argue with Robert Lowell, who had been one of the Bollingen judges. Angrily, Schwartz accused Lowell of being an anti-Semite, too; and Mizener, retailing all this for the Nabokovs' guests, said that he had to sympathize with Lowell because Cal was an honourable man, and so forth. Host Nabokov, who had been listening at some remove, suddenly paled and tugged at the sleeve of another guest, Professor M. H. Abrams, pulling him around the corner and out of the room. 'What am I going to do, Mike?' asked the stricken Nabokov. 'Arthur is a friend of mine but I am going to have to throw him out of my house.' 'Why?' asked Abrams, quite amazed. 'For telling that anti-Semitic story!' replied Nabokov. The statesmanship of M. H. Abrams prevailed, thereby preventing the realization of anything that might have resembled a scene that Nabokov would soon compose, the 'silent, soft, formless tussle on the part of two literati' – Humbert and Quilty, who, guessing his foreign-accented antagonist to be 'a German refugee', had reminded him, 'This is a Gentile's house, you know.' *That's* no joke, folks (as Hum would say). The incident at Nabokov's house is not funny, either; it is very touching.

The penultimate entry of *Pale Fire*'s Index, preceding '*Zembla*', is '*Yeslove*, a fine town, district and bishopric [a diocese; office of bishop – A.A.], north of Onhava, *149*, *275*'; and line 275 of the poem, we remember, reads: 'We have been married forty years' (John and Sybil Shade). Yes, love indeed; and it looks and sounds like a succinct allusion to Molly Bloom, I told Nabokov. 'Yes, it is,' he answered. 'My novel is a rather clever, complex thing, but its message is simple.' His words closely approximate what Joyce told Frank Budgen about *Ulysses*; and, nestled in the Index, Nabokov's 'message' is hidden in the requisite Joycean way.

Another well-kept secret at Cornell was the fact that Professor Nabokov was also a writer. I possessed this esoteric information, had read *The Real Life of Sebastian Knight* in 1953, as a sophomore; but this is neither the time nor the place to brag or strut. 'His style is even more florid than mine,' he announced one day, lecturing on Robert Louis Stephenson (as that difficult name is transliterated in my 1954 class notes) and *Dr Jekyll and Mr Hyde.* What does *that* mean? most of the class wondered. Was Stevenson a colourful lecturer, too? Not yet the best-selling author of *Lolita*, the celebrity prof whose enrolments would double, Nabokov was then beloved as a *teacher*; and he 'translated' and returned our warm esteem and gratitude in the only way a teacher should: by continuing to teach as well as he could. On a 1957 visit to Ithaca recorded in *Upstate* (1971), Edmund Wilson was horrified to see how hard Nabokov worked at his university job. When the hero of *Look at the Harlequins!* (1974) ponders the number of hours spent preparing two thousand pages of lectures, he is speaking for Nabokov. His *Eugene Onegin* translation and commentary (1964, revised 1975), the longest, most time-consuming project of his career (more than ten years), was begun at Véra's suggestion, in about 1950, as a service to his students, a modest mimeographed hand-out, a few stapled pages. It is most painful to think of this important collector's item, now buried in a box of college junk, mouldering in the basement or suburban garage of some ageing Cornell couple, unwanted, quite unloved.

Nabokov sometimes communicated his uncomplicated affection for his friends in terms quite literally of his own making. When introducing my wife and me to acquaintances in the hotel or friends from Montreux or nearby Vevey, Nabokov liked to tell them we had met in his lecture course. Actually, we did not; and she had, in fact, taken the course a year later than I. Given his dedication to the truth, whether perceived under or beyond the microscope, I finally corrected him one evening when he was happily talking about a letter he had received from 'another' couple who had met in that class. 'Of course you met in my class!' No. 'Véra, you remember, don't you?' She smiled, but offered no support. 'But I remember it so well,' he persisted. 'You were seated on opposite sides of the wide lecture hall. As the semester progressed you moved closer and closer. Finally, in the last week, the third on *Ulysses*, you were side by side.' No, I was sorry; this was not so. Different years. 'Really? I was *so* sure. Well, it is nevertheless a very beautiful story.' But he was certain that many couples had indeed met that way. I concurred – legions of doves, marching out of his last class two by two. He imagined one of 'his' couples on their first date discussing *Anna Karenina*, getting engaged, married, then naming their first child 'Anna'. 'I hope it was a daughter,' I said. 'Oh, yes, yes,' chortled Nabokov, his eyes starting to tear from his mirth. 'But if not, at least that troubled lad's Freudian shaman won't have to work too hard to discover the source of his "identity crisis". A few years, perhaps.'

Nabokov loved badinage, to him the conversational equivalent of tennis or one of those intentionally swift, and hence comical 'blitzkrieg' games of chess. Such sport was always in season. Witness our vacation with the Nabokovs in Zermatt in July 1974. I was walking down a side street with Nabokov, tap-tapping my furled umbrella on the cobblestones, when some unintentionally antic movement on my part caught his eye. 'Hmm,' mused Nabokov, 'a little gesture you just made with your umbrella and the way you are walking [gingerly, on wet stones] reminded me of Bob Hope in his first film, *Big Broadcast of* ... some year or other – we saw it in Paris before the war.' '*– of 1938*!', I declaimed, with a certain pride of pedantry, and then inquired, 'How did you know that was his first movie?' 'Ask me something I don't know,' responded Nabokov, surprised that I should be surprised by his scholarship. The implications of his challenge were clear. 'How many home runs did Babe Ruth hit in his career?' I asked (Hank Aaron had recently surpassed Ruth's record). Nabokov was astonished. 'Five hundred?' he inquired lamely, after several seconds. 'No,' I answered. 'Seven hundred and fourteen, not counting All-Star games and World Series.' 'Well, émigrés never know anything about baseball,' he said, with no conviction at all. The tide would soon turn in his favour; the fates smile ... and had this been said to him in conversation during our walk he would have glanced over at the deadpan comedian beside him, to pick up the smile or nuance of expression signalling temporary mental derangement, or 'Yes, the cliché cluster was intentional.' Nabokov detested and mocked clichés – most insidious as *poshlost*, that is, pretentious and deceptively 'serious' trash; but he did so not as a déclassé aristocrat or a 'correct usage' snob. Because clichés trivialize, betray or deny the uniqueness of the thought, memory or perception struggling to find expression, they are finally an affront to consciousness itself. 'How small the cosmos (a kangaroo's pouch would hold it), how paltry and puny in comparison to human consciousness, to a single individual recollection, and its expression in words!' Nabokov states in the first chapter of *Speak, Memory*, but not in the 1951 edition (then titled *Conclusive Evidence* [of his having existed]). He added that signal sentence when he was sixty-five, his eyes and mind ever open, alive, and Hopeful, to pun now in Quilty's manor and return us to the cobblestones of Zermatt.

Our visit to this Alpine town was to be a 'working vacation', as always for Nabokov, who even in his seventy-seventh year could be expected to walk and run ten to fifteen miles on a spring or summer day in search of butterflies. But it had rained the first two days of our stay in Zermatt. 'Oh, when will it clear, *when* will it clear?' groaned Nabokov, pacing the hotel lobby as though the world had been created the previous night, and he had to examine at once its resplendent marvels, describe and name them. On the third day there was light; and early that morning – far too early that morning – we accompanied the seventy-five-year-old writer-naturalist on a butterfly hunting trip ('lepping' he always called it) into the mountains. His sedentary guests walked along quite stoically, their thin-skinned office shoes no help at all, as amply soled Nabokov, squinting and scanning the horizon, talked on steadily, mainly about the flora and fauna around us. 'Tolstoy saw that [dense shrubbery] best' – these eyes, School of Nabokov, saw a black-green base splashed by brilliant orange flowers, a Fauvist bush – 'and you remember how Chekhov described those berries in – *ah*! There's one, what I've been looking for [name in Latin]'; and Nabokov was off, up and over some boulders, net aloft, an assault squad of one in pursuit of a pale-yellow butterfly. After depositing his capture ('Wonderful specimen, wonderful!') in the worn old Johnson & Johnson Band-Aid tin that had served him since the forties, the climb continued ('That hostel has the sweetest of Alpine butters, I speak as an expert, we can stop on the way down'), Nabokov's good spirits rising with the altitude, save for one quiet moment during our ascent when he paused on the path and gestured towards the hillside. 'This is the timberline of my youth. See those trees....' But his sentence trailed off (had he said 'aspens'?) and his pale blue eyes stared at and through the terra firma of Switzerland, fixed on a more distant and numinous space.

> The higher the dark and damp
> trails twist upward, the clearer
> grow the tokens, treasured since childhood,
> of my northern plain.
>
> Shall we not climb thus
> the slopes of paradise, at the hour of death,
> meeting all the loved things
> that in life elevated us?

wondered Nabokov in 'I Like That Mountain', a poem of 1925, composed in Feldberg (the Black Forest), when he was twenty-six. Now, here, almost fifty years later, the imperfect present tense; and Nabokov's ebullience was momentarily eclipsed or consumed by an inscrutable solitariness.

'Look, *I* caught a butterfly,' I proudly exclaimed a few minutes later, holding aloft the cupped hands that contained an insect I had picked off a very low shrub. 'Actually, that's a moth,' said Nabokov, his tone kind, almost apologetic. But I feigned humiliation, slumped abjectly, and the game was on. 'Moreover,' Nabokov added, with a mock frown, 'it is a common species.' I slumped even lower. [*Timidly*]: 'But I caught it with my bare hands.' 'Which is easy to do!' thundered Nabokov, his tone very dark now. 'They are drawn to the warmth of human hands' – he drew a breath, I slumped some more – 'and furthermore [theatrical pause before the final lethal thrust] this wingèd fellow was gaga from sleep.' I fell against a boulder and grabbed it for support as the bored and patient creature earned its freedom. The shimmering snow-walled Matterhorn behind me had provided an adequate backdrop for this genre scene, an old-fashioned *rencontre* in St Petersburg or Rio. '*Utterly defeated!*' proclaimed Nabokov, and we laughed.

Utterly defeated. That will never be said of Vladimir Nabokov, although McFate – as he jocularly named it in *Lolita* – too often tested and tormented him. His story – history? – is too well known to be rehearsed here.

> Beyond the seas where I have lost a sceptre,
> I hear the neighing of my dappled nouns,
> soft participles coming down the steps,
> treading on leaves, trailing their rustling gowns

Nabokov wrote in his finest American verse, 'An Evening of Russian Poetry' (1945), the year he became a US citizen. 'I haf nofing . . . I haf nofing left, nofing, nofing!' weeps addle-pated Timofey Pnin, the oldest Assistant Professor in the annals of American higher education. Yet Nabokov did not express himself that way. 'Few men who have lost so much have complained so little,' writes John Updike in his beautiful (unsigned) tribute to Nabokov in *The New Yorker* (18 July 1977). Again, an example: 'There was a period in the late 1920s when I used the courts of an elegant private club,' Nabokov told me in 1970, recalling the tennis lessons he gave as a very lean émigré in Berlin. ('Yes, six foot, 140 or so pounds,' eavesdropper Nabokov might say at this juncture, to deflate the potential pathos of my last phrase.) 'My pupils and I would wait for the "pro" and his German debutantes to depart for a long lunch – or whatever – and then we would use the court. More exactly, we'd arrive early to head off any rival poachers, and lurk behind trees, like spies or sporty detectives in an old film or *roman policier*, and once, when the pro – a blond brute – returned early, we had to run!'* He laughed as he spoke, restaging these scenes with no irony whatsoever, no hint of any kinship with the familiar formulas of a riches-to-rags-to-riches saga. These and other similar recollections were doubtless omitted from *Speak, Memory*

* Véra Nabokov, in a letter written to me in 1977, doubts that this occurred. It is 'completely and absolutely out of character. VN had pupils whom he taught English, who belonged to one of the best tennis clubs in Berlin, and who invited him to play there.' She wonders if VN said this (he did; I took notes afterwards) and suggests that, if he did, he must have been pulling my leg by paraphrasing the scene in *Lolita* in which Quilty takes advantage of Humbert's brief absence from the tennis court, and then, upon Humbert's return, drops the racket and runs. Simon Karlinsky's forthcoming edition of the Nabokov–Edmund Wilson correspondence will include a letter in which VN discusses the activities in America of a non-existent brother! The relatively small matter of the tennis caper implies much about the challenges and problems implicit in biography, a subject central to *The Real Life of Sebastian Knight.* Mr Goodman, Knight's comically inept biographer, has accepted as fact absurdities fed to him by Knight himself: 'Sebastian speaking of his very first novel (unpublished and destroyed) explained that it was about a fat young student who travels home to find his mother married to his uncle; this uncle, an ear-specialist, has murdered the student's father. Mr. Goodman misses the joke.' To what extent do biographers and memoirists belong to Mr Goodman's party?

lest they appear to limn self-pity or confuse significant experience with the demands and vagaries of business and low finance. I've said nothing about genius, a miraculous or perhaps preternatural force. Dignity, honour, character, courage, tenacity, and a transcendent sense of humour, these are some of the representative and recognizable *human* qualities responsible for Nabokov's massive and darkling oeuvre, his gift to us.

The amplitude of Nabokov's resilient spirit is summarized for me by one further recollection of Cornell, when I was one of thirty or so students enrolled in his Russian Literature course. The class was held at the end of a long, windowless, dimly lit corridor in the basement of Goldwin Smith Hall, one side of which was devoted to the Art Department's motley and dusty collection of plaster-of-Paris Greek sculpture, artifacts and architectural fragments. I was rushing to class one dismal wintry morning, three or four minutes late, but slackened my stride when I noticed that Professor Nabokov was also late, and walking ahead of me half-way down the hall. He hurried into a classroom, and my heart quopped (one of VN's favourite coinages in *Ulysses*, very impressive when worked into an exam answer or fraternity conversation) as I realized it was one door too soon. I entered the class to find Professor Nabokov several sentences into his lecture; not wanting to waste another minute, he was stooped over his notes, intently reading them to thirty stunned students, a shell-shocked platoon belonging to an even tardier don. Trying to be as transparent as possible, I approached the lectern and touched Nabokov on the sleeve. He turned, and peered down at me over his eyeglasses, amazed. 'Mr Nabokov,' I said very quietly, 'you are in the wrong classroom.' He readjusted his glasses on his nose, focused his gaze on the motionless frieze-like figures seated before him, and calmly announced, 'You have just seen the "Coming Attraction" for Literature 325. If you are interested, you may register next fall.' Professor Pnin no more, he closed his folder of notes and moved one door down the dark hall. 'A most extraordinary thing has just happened, most extraordinary,' he told the students of Literature 325, chuckling to himself as he opened his folder once more and, not bothering to explain what had happened, began to lecture.

That spirit and the support and iron-willed confidence of Véra, his wife for more than half a century, sustained Vladimir Nabokov, allowing talent and genius to prevail. He was fifty-four at the time of this incident, the shortest-lived and least traumatic displacement of his long exile. *Lolita*, *Pnin*, *Pale Fire*, the four-volume Pushkin edition, *Ada*, and much much more, were not yet born, not to mention the baker's dozen of his untranslated Russian works – in English, a lucky thirteen. Yet Nabokov's memories of his luckless generation of Russian writers were for the most part circumscribed by gloom. He might speak of Vladislav Khodasevich, say, with keen admiration, but sadly, as if he knew, miraculously, that hardly anyone now reading this page would recognize the name of that extraordinary poet and critic (1886–1939). After dinner one evening, during our November 1972 visit to Montreux, I showed Nabokov an early version of the table of contents for *The Bitter Air of Exile*: *Russian Writers in the West, 1922–72*, which I was co-editing with Simon Karlinsky (the title is drawn from a poem by Anna Akhmatova). He studied the pages, silently, visibly moved by the idea of an anthology in English devoted to these writers, part of that 'mythical tribe whose bird-signs and moon-signs [Nabokov] retrieve[s] from the desert dust' in *The Gift*, to quote his Foreword to that great novel. 'So nice, so very nice,' he said softly, placing the pages on the table between us. At 4 a.m., when I arose for a glass of water (I'm a decorous reporter), I could hear someone pacing the floor above us in the Nabokovs' apartment. The next morning he handed me an index card. 'The product of my insomnia,' he said. 'You may use it as an epigraph for your Tsvetaeva section, or however you wish.' The card contained his translation of several unidentified lines by Marina Tsvetaeva, whom he had known in Paris during the thirties. 'A poet of genius,' he says of her in *Speak, Memory*. Tsvetaeva endured extreme poverty, isolation, illness, political disgrace (because of her husband, a double agent) and finally committed suicide in 1941 – a terrible story, not untypical of émigré life. The verse Nabokov chose for us reads:

> Amidst the dust of bookshops, wide dispersed
>   And never purchased there by anyone,
> Yet similar to precious wines, my verse
>   Can wait: its turn shall come.

Landless, utterly free, wielding a new 'sceptre', Nabokov in the last fifteen years of his life triumphed on the international scale of Stravinsky and Balanchine, fellow émigrés who did not have to perform in another language. Speaking at the memorial service for Vladimir Nabokov in New York on 21 July 1977, Dmitri Nabokov said that his father, on a final walk with him in the mountains, had spoken happily of his life's accomplishment: 'As Schopenhauer might have imagined it, my father's books, he told me, were like an undeveloped film that gradually came into life.' Thus the final visual trope of a writer who shared a few vistas with Ansel Adams, and who did, alas, leave one secret negative, in Dmitri's words 'the last photograph of that film': *The Original of Laura*, a novel in progress, one-third completed, 'secret' because Nabokov abhorred the posthumous publication of an author's unfinished work.

Nabokov's contentment was surely predicated on a confident sense that the subtle and glowing pigments of thousands upon thousands of inimitable sentences and paragraphs will indeed prove durable. The 'aurochs' alluded to in the closing sentences of *Lolita* (my epigraph) refer to those delicate and stylized images of bison, those early Klees, still visible on the cave walls of France and Spain where they were painted ten to twenty thousand years ago. So-called posterity, obviously enough, will decide whether or not Nabokov possessed 'the secret' of which Humbert speaks; time will tell, as a platitudinous reviewer might say.

But, for now, do the following six miniature enchantments need any signatures in order to be identified as 'Nabokovs'? From *The Gift*: 'Pattern of Elysian hues! Once in Ordos [China] my father, climbing a hill after a storm, inadvertently entered the base of a rainbow – the rarest occurrence! – and found himself in colored air, in a play of light as if in paradise. He took one more step – and left paradise.' Fyodor, *The Gift*'s apprentice poet, also says, 'I am convinced that extraordinary surprises await us [in death]. It's a pity one can't imagine what one can't compare to anything. Genius is an African who dreams up snow.' In *Pnin*, an equivalent genius flourishes on another continent, when a young artist dreams of placing various objects in turn behind a glass of water: 'The comb, stood on end, resulted in the glass's seeming to fill with beautifully striped liquid, a zebra cocktail.' Conversely, a summoning in *Speak, Memory* of the worn-down coloured pencils of Nabokov's idyllic childhood concludes with an invisible image, a quantum leap towards infinite reaches: 'The white one alone, that lanky albino among pencils, kept its original length, or at least did so until I discovered that, far from being a fraud leaving no mark on the page, it was the ideal implement since I could imagine whatever I wished while I scrawled' (see the dazzling digression on a pencil which constitutes Chapter 3, *Transparent Things*). Or, lest we overlook Nabokov's aural surprises, here is another literally narrow and slender example, or wooden passage, of a kind more necessary than ever to a culture drawn to the sensibilities of Clint Eastwood, Sam Peckinpah, punk rock, et al.: 'With the help of the janitor [Pnin] screwed onto the side of the desk a pencil sharpener – that highly satisfying, highly philosophical implement that goes ticonderoga-ticonderoga, feeding on the yellow finish and sweet wood, and ends up in a kind of soundlessly spinning ethereal void as we all must.' As Professor Nabokov said in class, more than once, only a sibilant separates 'comic' and 'cosmic'. The wake, it appears, is over; who is smiling now as we contemplate that glide, no longer rhetorical, towards the – void? 'Death is divestment, death is communion,' states the authorial voice in the opening chapter of *Pnin*. 'It may be wonderful to mix with the landscape, but to do so is the end of the tender ego.'

A few days before Nabokov's death, when his son Dmitri was leaving the hospital room, he noticed tears in his father's eyes, indicating that Vladimir Nabokov knew that he would never go in quest of butterflies again. Fifty years earlier, in Berlin, Vladimir Nabokov, aged twenty-eight, revised and expanded the sunny concluding vision of 'I Like That Mountain' (1925) by writing this poem, titled 'In Paradise' ('V rayu', translated by the author in *Poems and Problems*, 1970):

My soul, beyond distant death
your image I see like this:
a provincial naturalist,
an eccentric lost in paradise.

There, in a glade, a wild angel slumbers,
a semi-pavonian creature.
Poke at it curiously
with your green umbrella,

speculating how, first of all,
you will write a paper on it,
then – But there are no learned journals,
nor any readers in paradise!

And there you stand, not yet believing
your wordless woe.
About that blue somnolent animal
whom will you tell, whom?

Remembering Nabokov

Where is the world and the labeled roses,
the museum and the stuffed birds?
And you look through your tears
at those unnamable wings.

3 Mr Nabokov

Hannah Green

Towards the end of the Second World War and after it for three or four years, Vladimir Nabokov taught at Wellesley College, where I was a student. He taught courses in the Russian language beginning with beginning grammar (he was himself the entire Russian Department), and he taught a survey of Russian Literature in translation – Russian 201. It was in this course that I enrolled in my junior year. I forget now what lucky chance led me to decide on it – perhaps I knew that if I took it I would really read *War and Peace.* At any rate, I went through college on the adage 'Choose your courses for the professors', and Mr Nabokov had a special reputation as a teacher: there were more than a hundred girls attending Russian 201.

He was about forty-five then, and he was almost unknown as a writer in this country. I had the blue paper-covered book, little-magazine size, put out by New Directions, called *Nine Stories.* It had a big N on the cover – for 'Nine' or for 'Nabokov' – and I carried it around with me and occasionally dipped into its mystifying pages. I loved the feel of it; I considered it exotic. I did not know about *Despair* or *The Real Life of Sebastian Knight*; I did not even come across his book on Gogol until four or five years later and read it then, as I did *Conclusive Evidence*, in a state of rapture.

One evening during that winter we took Russian 201, Mr Nabokov gave a reading of his poems. I recall the atmosphere of excitement – the warmth, the darkness of the hall, and Mr Nabokov far down there (I had come too late to sit up close), his face lit by the lamp of the lectern. There was an air of occasion about it all. His wife was there, sitting in the centre of the front row. I could see the back of the head of her to whom his love poems were addressed – and from time to time between poems I could hear the shuffle of papers and the sounds of their two voices as he bent forward to discuss something briefly.

But, still, at the time we studied Russian Literature with him we did not think of him as a writer or as a poet, though we knew, of course, that he was both and that he was distinguished; to us he was Mr

Nabokov, he was our teacher, and we found him dashing and extraordinary. He dazzled our minds and instilled in us feelings of the most exalted romance – not with him, but with Russian literature, and with the history and the land (the geography) in which it was, he showed us, inextricably involved.

Sarah Johns, my favourite friend, and I used to dash from Beebe Hall ahead of everyone else after lunch and dance all the way down the hill until we arrived at the back path that led up the hill to Sage, the building with the big lecture hall in which Mr Nabokov gave his course. We liked to go up the log-and-earth steps of that narrow path and past the big old oak and then around the building in order to arrive at the front door at just the same time as Mr Nabokov, so we could greet him coming in.

He was tall and thickly, loosely built, with brown hair and somewhat dry, ruddy, weathered skin, and he had a large, well-formed face. His high forehead had a series of lines. His aura was one of casual, relaxed manliness. He had the pleasing smell of a man who smokes, and an air of a certain diffidence, of a natural aristocratic dignity; and he was, I realize now, the first teacher I ever had who was at home in literature, for he was himself a part of it.

I see him still, standing in the sunlight outside Sage on an ice-cold winter day in his handsome brown tweed jacket, a wool scarf around his neck, for even on the coldest day of winter he never wore an overcoat. That was the most intimate fact we knew about him – that and the fact that sometimes he had headaches and then his wife came to class in his stead and read his lecture for the day.

She was beautiful, with long, thick, glossy white hair falling almost to her shoulders and very smooth, radiant pink-white skin. She read his lectures carefully, slowly, with an accent; and she wrote the words with which she thought we might have difficulty in huge, foot-high letters on the blackboard. In two days he would be back again, talking (it seemed), not reading, telling us everything as if it had only at that moment marvellously occurred to him to say it that way.

His words, his wonderful words! I heard every word he said, and I wrote down as much as I could. I had a terrible time in those years because, usually, though I fiercely willed it not to happen, no sooner would a lecture or a classroom discussion begin than my mind would fly out the window and remain beyond earshot up in the trees, dreaming whatever it wished; try as I would by holding my head up, shifting positions, pinching myself, propping up my eyelids with my fingers, I could not concentrate on what I so longed to learn. Not so with Mr Nabokov. My mind was there the whole time and enthralled. Even now I remember some of the things he said. He spoke of Turgenev's sentences as being 'long and low and curved up on the ends like lizards' tails'. He said that Turgenev was the first to write about slaves who were superior to their masters (and he went to jail and was then exiled to his estate for that), the first to write well about babies and about dogs – dogs that smiled, the way dogs lie down.

He said, 'Read and dream through Chekhov's bleak landscapes, which convey a dim loveliness and are like gray clothes on a gray clothesline flapping against a gray sky.' He said, 'Chekhov's world is dove-gray.'

He described the 'liquid-blue world of' – was it Lomonosov? There was too much for me to hold it all, and though my ardent mind took in everything he said, I seem to remember first the gayer things he said for fun. At one moment he would speak with the most profound and elegant seriousness, and at the next he would recall that we were college girls and had to have the 'world' of each writer defined for the sake of memorizing. Everything he told us was lit by the flashes of his own peculiar genius, and he shared with us the light of his own knowledge – the details and facts that he loved.

He told us he pronounced *Eugene Onegin Eugene One-Gin* in English. He went painstakingly through the translation of 'Eugene One-Gin' in the anthology we had, and he corrected certain lines for us. We rewrote those lines in our books in pencil. He told us to. He said that of all the Russian writers Pushkin loses the most in translation. He spoke of the 'zooming music' of his poetry, and of the wonderful rhythm, of how 'the oldest epithets are rejuvenated in Pushkin's verse', which 'bubbles and gleams in the darkness'. He spoke of the wonderful development of plot in *Eugene One-Gin*, which Pushkin took ten years to write, of the retrospective and introspective rambling of the plot. And he read aloud for us the duel in *Eugene One-Gin*, in which One-Gin mortally wounds the poet Lenski. In this scene, Mr Nabokov said, Pushkin foretold his own death.

He drew a diagram to scale on the blackboard so that we would be able to see exactly the shape and size of the duelling ground on which Pushkin was shot by the Frenchman d'Anthès. He explained the form of the duel. He set the scene – an ice-cold January afternoon (27 January 1837) on a hill in the suburbs of St Petersburg. Dusk was already in the air. The banks of the frozen Neva were covered with snow, and Pushkin's wife, whose whims were indirectly the cause of the duel, had gone sledding. She was a dazzling beauty, a slant-eyed madonna, frivolous, insignificant, a flirt, cold, bored by Pushkin's poems, and a great success at court, to which Pushkin had been condemned, for Tsar Nicholas I had decided to make himself Pushkin's censor. (Though Pushkin never left Russia, he drank his fill of banishment, Mr Nabokov said, and Pushkin thought and said that government curbs made exiles of writers. Pushkin hated the despotism of the Tsar and of public opinion.) Mr Nabokov told us who the seconds were and described their function. He drew the lines of the *barrière*, defined by cloaks on the snow, and described Pushkin and d'Anthès, who had been flirting with Pushkin's wife and had less than a month before married her sister, approaching each other from a distance of twenty paces, their pistols loaded. It was exactly 4.30. D'Anthès fired first, and Pushkin fell, mortally wounded in the stomach. He managed, however, to raise himself up, call d'Anthès to the *barrière*, and shoot. The blow from his bullet, which hit d'Anthès's arm, caused him to fall, and Pushkin, thinking he had killed him, shouted 'Bravo!' Two days later, Pushkin, the greatest of the Russian poets, died. He was thirty-six. In the night his body was taken in a coffin to a monastery.

(Reading Mr Nabokov's commentary on *Eugene Onegin* recently, I concluded that he must have omitted certain of the details which had brought about the duel because he considered them unfit for our college-girl ears.)

Early the second semester, Mr Nabokov told us he had graded the Russian writers, and we must write down their grades in our notebooks and learn them by heart: Tolstoy was A-plus. Pushkin and Chekhov were A. Turgenev A-minus. Gogol was B-minus. And Dostoevsky was C-minus. (Or was he D-plus?) As the year went on, he made us understand the reasons for his judgements. 'He who prefers Dostoevsky to Chekhov,' he said, 'will never understand the essentials of Russian life.'

He didn't talk about conflict or symbols or character development. He did not talk about the things that were usually talked about in literature courses. He did not try to make us state the underlying meaning of something. He did not make us talk about *themes*. He never took the joy out of reading. He spoke of the way certain characters in Gogol nod vividly into his pages and disappear never to appear again. 'How charming that is,' he said, and he read aloud to us a passage about a certain blue-eyed, red-faced policeman who appeared on a certain page of our edition of *Dead Souls*, and disappeared never to reappear.

He said of Chekhov, 'No other author has created such pathetic creatures.' He said, 'Learn by heart "The Ravine", "The Duel", "The Lady with the Little Dog".' He spent several days going through 'The Lady with the Little Dog', pointing out things of which we ought to take note, for they were characteristic of Chekhov's art. Summing up, he said:

1. Note how the story is told in the most natural way possible, slowly, without break, in a subdued voice.
2. Note how characterization is achieved by the selection and distribution of refined details.
3. Note that there is neither moral nor message.
4. Note how the story's movement is based on a system of waves, on shades of this or that mood. Note the contrast of poetry and prose. For Chekhov, the lofty and the base are points of the beauty and the pity of the world.
5. Note how the storyteller goes out of his way to allude to trifles that are meaningless to the action and have no symbolic meaning but are important for the atmosphere. And
6. Note that the story does not end. The final scene is full of pathos. The two lovers are the closest of couples, the best of friends. There is no solution in a typical Chekhovian story – the story fades out like life; there is no end, for as long as there is life there is no possible conclusion to troubles.

He told us what a lovable man Chekhov was, how kind and how simple. He loved the sincere. Everybody loved him. The radicals criticized Chekhov for not actively espousing their cause, but he was an artist, an individualist; he served the people and their causes in his own way. In 1890, Chekhov went to Sakhalin and wrote of the horrible conditions there. Tolstoy loved Chekhov dearly.

Mr Nabokov talked of what Tolstoy did with *time* in *War and Peace*. How exact the illusion of time! Tolstoy set the clock of the novel to keep time with the watch of the reader, and he achieved in this way a perfect rhythm.

He talked about Tolstoy's women. 'How wonderful they are!...

Observe them carefully,' he said. 'Imagine them as vividly as possible.' He talked about the Rostov family, about Natasha, whom Tolstoy modelled after his wife and her sister, about Sonya, modelled after his Aunt Volkonsky. He talked about Prince Andrey and Pierre. To Prince Andrey Tolstoy gave his own energy, his vigour and distinction, but to Pierre he gave his soul.

Mr Nabokov described Tolstoy as a passionate moralist, obsessed by the quest for truth. The reader must sometimes follow him unwillingly, for 'Russian truth is not a comfortable companion – not the everyday *pravda* but the immortal *istina*, which is the very soul of truth. When found, *istina* is the splendour of the creative imagination.' No other author has been able to make artistic truth and people mingle as Tolstoy did in *War and Peace.* Tolstoy himself is invisible in the book. Like God, he is nowhere and everywhere.

Unconsciously, Tolstoy was on the right path, Mr Nabokov said. But Tolstoy, who felt things more deeply than most men, had a supersensitive, superhuman consciousness, and in his fifth decade his conscience led him to give up fiction. He would not let his conscience strike a bargain with his lower nature, and he suffered for it. He thought his art ungodly because it was based on imagination. When he had reached creative perfection, he decided not to write fiction. He sacrificed the artist to the philosopher. He said that all he had written was falsehood, that only God could create. But he remained an artist at heart, and towards the end of his life he was unable to chain his gigantic creative need. His last stories were untainted by deliberate moralizing. He had found that truth cannot be preached; it must be discovered.

Tolstoy wanted to write a sequel to *War and Peace*, to go on with Pierre and Natasha and history. Pierre would join the Decembrist movement. In the fragment he wrote, Natasha has followed Pierre to Siberia. She is an old lady when she comes home. Her dark eyes gazing into the distance, she sits in a room resting from the whole life-love she has lived through. Nothing more is to be expected. She has spent herself and is pale and sad. There is majesty, grace, love. Tolstoy weaves heavenly roses into Russian life.

So Mr Nabokov spoke. Sometimes he read poems to us in Russian and he told us to listen to the sounds, for these could not be captured in translation. He read some of the poems of Fet aloud to us and then read his own translations. 'Real verse music is not the melody of the verse,' he said. 'Authentic verse music is that mystery which brims over the rational texture of the line.'

He spoke of the great lyric poet Tyutchev, who had been neglected for decades because he was politically conservative (he was not very intelligent politically), but who saw and made his readers see 'the golden oil of moon on waters'. He spoke of Tyutchev's incandescent genius, which was Russian through and through.

Once, to our great delight, Mr Nabokov drew a butterfly for us on the blackboard. It was much larger than life-size, perfectly rendered, with all its minute details – antennae, eyes, and the charming pattern of its wings.

In the gayest, most natural, most charming way in the world, he opened the door and led us into the world of Russian literature. He taught us to take literature seriously and what is ordinarily said about it lightly. He gave me back my passion for reading.

During spring vacation I read *War and Peace* day after day, all day long, sitting in the book-lined study of our house in Ohio, and when I was finished I threw the book down on the floor and myself down on top of it and I wept with my face against the book. I wept for the book, and I wept because it was over and now I would have to come back into my real life again. I was desolate.

I still have that copy of *War and Peace* – time-worn and rain-warped and soft, with underlinings in the pale-purple ink that I used in those days – frequent at the start and then, gradually, as I became disembodied, absorbed into the book, disappearing altogether.

I see us as we were that winter: Sarah Johns and Trudy Knowlton and me sitting together side by side in the front row of the big lecture hall as close as we could get to Mr Nabokov, and the others scattered through the upward-sloping hall – fifty or so girls, mostly juniors and seniors – all of us peeling off our heavy coats, our mittens, our scarves and hats, sitting there with our green spiral notebooks, in our plaid skirts and sweaters over white blouses with Peter Pan collars, wearing our thick white wool socks (bobby socks, but we did not know that word then) and brown leather Weejuns or white-and-brown saddle shoes, listening, taking notes, our legs crossed, Sarah's lovely radiant face pressed forward, listening to Mr Nabokov.

When the lecture was over, the bell rang, and everyone got up and tramped out. I remember the thudding sounds of some hundred feet and thinking, how *dull* they are, they think he's not serious, while we three sat on enchanted, not wanting to leave.

'We want to hear it over again,' we said. 'We want to hear more.' He smiled, pleased, but gathered up his papers and gently departed without saying anything further.

At the end of the year, when June had come and exams were over and the leaves were green and the days were hot, and we three were about to part for the summer, we were walking along together following the narrow back path down the hill behind Sage and we met Mr Nabokov coming up the path. We stopped agog, bashfully, to greet him.

'One of you did very well,' he said.

'One of you did very well, one of you did very well' – it sang in my mind, resounding; it made the blood rush to my head in pleasure and delight, not only because I knew it was I who had done very well but also because he knew that I was one of us three.

I suppose Mr Nabokov did not take us seriously. Certainly he did not take us personally. After all, we were college girls. No doubt it was we who inspired Humbert Humbert's extreme distaste for the lot of us.

And yet he gave us the best, and I imagine his true attitude towards us – towards the lot of us – was one of gentle dismay, a kind of tenderness and a kind of helplessness in the face of the fact of the worlds that separated our minds from his, a bemused acceptance of what fate had dealt him: American college girls. All this was combined with a determination to go on singing, to go on telling everything that was sacred to him in the Russia he had lost and in its literature and in its language. He would go on doing this whether or not we could really hear him. He would go on doing it in a language not his own even as he expressed it in the poem 'An Evening of Russian Poetry'. It is a sad poem, a graceful poem, beautiful and affecting, kind, humorous – a poem of exile, a love poem to his lost Russia, a poem with that true verse music of which he spoke in connection with the poet Fet – the melodies of sorrow, of longing, of human delight, which brim mysteriously over the rational texture of lines of this poet, Mr Nabokov, whose plight is that he must address himself for ever to Sylvia, to Emmy, to Cynthia, to Joan.

4 Under Cover of Decadence: Nabokov as Evangelist and Guide to the Russian Classics

John Bayley

Nabokov's critical principles are as original as his creative work, as ambiguous, and on occasion as perverse. Were we to take him seriously, or earnestly rather, we should have to conclude him to be some sort of decadent, both in his own writing and in his literary tastes. By decadent I mean an artist who, while not necessarily corrupt or cruel, sensational or over-ingenious, is liable to make such an impression, in his evident wish to secure certain sorts of novel or striking effect. In any age there can be decadent artists in this sense, artists who are reacting against that which has become too much taken for granted in the name of art. They reject any commonplace idea of 'human interest', of the permanent and universal effect of art to which, as Dr Johnson said, 'every bosom returns an echo'.

Decadent art must startle us, but this originality is apt to be self-defeating. Successful decadent art can be recognized by the stability and reliability of the product. It has done just what it set out to do. Tolstoy defined unsuccessful decadent art when he observed that the trouble with much modern writing, as he had experienced it around the mid-nineties in the course of writing *What is Art?*, is that one saw just what the artist intended and one was soon bored by it. If we see the point and are bored by it, then the thing has not come off: if we see the point and feel what Nabokov once called 'aesthetic bliss', then it has. The impact is definitive; the effect of the decadent work of art necessarily limited by its own kind of originality. It says one thing – its own thing – to us; and, whether successful or not, this is too idiosyncratic to join up with the larger fund of human and aesthetic interest implicit in all great art. The distinction cannot, of course, be an absolute one; but it serves to indicate the area of aesthetic judgement concerned, one that is more easily demonstrated in the visual arts than in writing. A Klimt, say, or an Odilon Redon is as elegantly in charge of a specified area as is a first-class detective story or a certain sort of Hellenic statue; and, if we admit this, it is equally clear that a Vuillard or a Klee, a Mondrian or a Jackson Pollock, however seemingly specialized in technique and purpose, in fact leads us subtly into a dimension and a perspective that widens not only into the world of common experience but into all other visions of it. However idiosyncratic, they are not decadent. In a less evident way a story by Borges or Andreyev could be called decadent, while an equally *raffiné* narration of Henry James, Kipling, John Updike or L. P. Hartley, would not be. A narration by Nabokov himself? That question might be at least partially answered by attention to Nabokov's views on other authors – and in particular Russian authors – as well as to the productions of his own talent.

He frequently tells us, directly and indirectly, that his favourite Russians – Pushkin and Gogol and, to a lesser extent, Lermontov – are creators of pure art, of 'aesthetic bliss'. They have created a world in which only fatuous or sinister philistines, do-gooders, Soviet critics, professorial lackeys of the Writers' Union, earnest American sophomores, will attempt to detect social, political, or moral relevance. No message can be found, no 'human values' should be emphasized. By contrast such things may be more or less relevant in discussing Turgenev; and 'those who think Turgenev a great writer' are welcome to the use of them.

The casual thrust, negligently interposed in parenthesis during the marvellously detailed notes to the translation of Pushkin's *Eugene Onegin*, is typical of the way Nabokov makes his points. Subtle, intricate and joyful art scorns to be other than itself, and scorns to be joined on to the general procession of human experience. Thus Nabokov is claiming for it what is by fairly general consent true of the art of decadence. For Nabokov great art is magic music, magic words. Shakespeare, the greatest verbal magician, the genius more Pushkin than Pushkin, the artist from whose sun so much pale fire has been snatched, is specifically enclosed inside this magic corral.

But great art is not in this sense magical; at any rate, magic is not the effect aimed at, and not the effect obviously achieved. An art of magic is naturally coarse – 'rough magic' is Shakespeare's seemingly conscious phrase in *The Tempest* – because it must strike us at once as singular and remarkable: it never strikes us the less at first, as used to be said of Raphael, to impress us the more surely later on. Of course, Shakespeare and Pushkin, like Titian and Velazquez, could do both things, as all their seasoned clients realize; but Shakespeare and Pushkin have far more to offer their client, as he develops and as he re-reads them, than they offer at the first assay.

And, of course, Nabokov knew this perfectly well. But he disliked so much the critical stance that goes with finding socially significant types and situations in the work of such masters as Pushkin and Gogol that he affects to fall back on the simple and seductive criteria of decadent art. It was very natural he should do so. During wartime he had become a refugee from Europe and its political and ideological divisions; and he had then found himself in an America that had been conditioned to read literature in the spirit of uplift and earnestness. Moreover, he had behind him the ideas of the early Russian formalists, which maintained that the meaning of the work is simply the way in which it is written, and that a perception of the form revealed the content. The formalists were fascinated by *Tristram Shandy*, the classic instance of a novel whose function was to be itself. Oddly enough, the theories of formalism did not openly conflict, after the revolution, with the crude doctrines of socialist realism; partly because formalism, like mathematics, was not concerned with ideology at all, and partly because the notion of understanding a work of art in this way was not so very different from the way in which Marxism laid down the conditions for understanding society. In any event, Viktor Shklovsky, the venerable founding father of formalist ideas, is still alive and well, living in the Soviet Union.

Nabokov is no more concerned with formalism than with any other 'ism'. Nor was formalism concerned with the spirit and ideas of 'la Décadence'. And yet they shared a common *Zeitgeist*; and Nabokov shared it too. It was in the air of Berlin, when he was living there and writing under the pen-name of Sirin; and it is just as evident in one of his last novels, *Ada*, as in *Mary*, his first. The comedy of *Pale Fire* is an elaboration of the comedy in *Tristram Shandy*. And *Tristram Shandy*, as Shklovsky himself went to some lengths to show, is by far the most important influence on the method of *Eugene Onegin*, much more so than the Byronic influence. *Eugene Onegin* is a Shandean novel rather than a 'Don-Juan'-style poem.

Nabokov perceived this too; and it is one reason for the delight he takes in Pushkin. The title *Pale Fire* is itself a joke that reveals his innate modesty. Pushkin and Gogol are for him not only the great Russian masters, but the masters whose inspiration can descend to and inhabit a lesser and later writer. From their suns he can snatch his own pale fire. And he wishes his own works to be read as he himself read theirs: '... by poetry I mean the mysteries of the irrational as perceived through rational words. True poetry of that kind provokes

– not laughter and not tears – but a radiant smile of perfect satisfaction, a purr of beatitude – and a writer may well be proud of himself if he can make his readers, or more exactly some of his readers, smile and purr that way.' That quotation from his short book on Gogol – the best thing in English written on Gogol – tells its own story. What Nabokov understands by poetry is not 'verse', but the verbal saturation that gives us 'the mysteries of the irrational as revealed through rational words'. In this sense Gogol's novel *Dead Souls* is a poem – Gogol actually referred to it as a *poema* – just as Pushkin's poem *Eugene Onegin* is a novel. And the goal and achievement of such poetry is to provoke a purr of beatitude – the state of aesthetic bliss – and no mere vulgar human responses like laughter and tears.

But why not both? Are not the two compatible? In practice Nabokov knows perfectly well that they are; but his point is that an emphasis on anything relating to the tears-and-laughter side of things leads to bad criticism, to misunderstanding, to the true artistic inspiration and technique of the work being bypassed or ignored. It leads to Gogol being praised for Dickensian pathos or for devastating social criticism. Nabokov's suggestion is not that we should be heartless, that we should refuse to be 'touched' or 'moved', but that we should dispense with the heart and the tear-ducts in order to understand and enter into the kind of aesthetic joyfulness that really animates such 'poetry'. That we should dispense, above all, with the obstinate notion that the denizens of such poetry are 'real' persons, linked with our own lives and experiences, and 'standing for' something of importance in the history of human consciousness that has helped to shape our own lives and make them comprehensible to us.

Nabokov is amused and exasperated at the fact that – as he sees it – a work saturated by the kind of 'poetry' he loves is also liable to attract the attention of critics who must at all cost find a 'meaning' in it. He implies that they must have such a meaning because *they* are exasperated, without knowing they are, by the beautiful independence from all such meanings of the aesthetic and poetic structure of his favourite works. Such persons want to locate a character and a meaning in what he calls 'the dream-play' of Hamlet, because they cannot obtain the proper and full satisfaction from the aesthetic rapture of the Hamlet experience. *Hamlet*, says Nabokov, is not a 'tragedy', any more than Gogol's and Pushkin's masterpieces are. O'Neill's *Mourning Becomes Electra* is one, because tragic meaning is what it laboriously sets out to give us. Similarly, Gogol's comedy *Revizor*, *The Government Inspector* – Nabokov prefers to translate it as a 'dreamplay' titled *Government Spectre* – is not a comedy in the dismal sense that 'Molière's stuff' is: that it a play with a social point to make. 'A bad play is more apt to be good comedy or good tragedy than the incredibly complicated creations of such men as Shakespeare and Gogol.'

Nabokov's objection is indeed a decidedly cogent one, and the more so because he does not bother to guard himself against the kind of misunderstanding it can give rise to. The critical *bien pensant* looks down his nose and calls him a heartless aesthete, a kind of preserved dandy from the nineties whose view of art and its function is hopelessly old-fashioned. But what he is attacking is the critical attitude that seeks to *place* a work of art, its intention, tendency and significance, as if it were a relatively simple and polemical tract. Any such interpretation of the works he is talking about is, in fact, liable to suggest: the art stops here – where it has made its point, said what it has to say, performed its function in terms of humanity. Paradoxically, therefore, Nabokov's aesthetic is doing just the opposite of what it appears to be doing. Instead of affirming the closed circle of decadent effectiveness, the area of complete – and therefore limited – satisfaction, it is suggesting that a great artistic achievement stops nowhere; and that its perfections have no relation to its endlessly appreciable and variable self, but only to the feelings it arouses in us and the kinds of pleasure it gives.

Onegin himself probably owes as much to Hamlet as the construction of the verse-novel does to *Tristram Shandy*. Onegin is a method rather than a person, but a method a great part of the effectiveness of which consists in arranging for him to become a controversial character. Onegin is less human than Hamlet because the method shows more, more scintillatingly, with more deliberate openness. Pushkin observes that there is something wrong with him, which is natural enough in someone who is an ingenious device and parody rather than a person; and this observation is not only disarming: it sets the reader off on a fool's errand. What is this malady, 'the cause of which it's high time were discovered'? Nabokov disposes of the question pungently: 'To this quest Russian critics have applied themselves with tremendous zeal, accumulating in the course of a dozen decades one of the most boring masses of comments known to civilised man. Even a special term for Onegin's distemper has been invented (*Oneginstvo*,

'Oneginism'); and thousands of pages have been devoted to him as a "type" of something or other.' The favourite type was of the 'superfluous man', the man of ideals and education whom the social evils of despotism had paralysed, not only in terms of action but of feeling and thought as well:

Thus a character borrowed from books but recomposed by a great poet to whom life and library were one, placed by that poet within a brilliantly reconstructed environment, and played with ... in a succession of compositional patterns – lyrical impersonations, tomfooleries of genius, literary parodies, and so on – is treated by Russian pedants as a sociological and historical phenomenon typical of Alexander I's regime (alas this tendency to generalise and vulgarise the unique fancy of an individual genius has also its advocates in the United States).

But, of course, the pedants are right too. In their own way pedants recognize a great work of art no less unerringly than Nabokov himself. For what pedant spends his time spinning historical and social significance out of the wholly limited effectiveness of a decadent work? The privilege and perhaps the burden of a great work is to attract comment of all kinds – the stupid and opinionated as well as the perceptive and enthusiastic. Would Nabokov himself wish it otherwise? His *Lolita* was hailed in America as a piece of profound social and historical criticism, the apotheosis in art not only of the phenomenon of American female precocity, but of the gulf between traditional European romantic love and the new American sexuality. 'Rubbish,' said Nabokov; but he must have known he was being paid the compliment – however backhanded a one – that goes to great artists; that goes to Shakespeare when some pretentious ass of a producer tells us that 'the real subject of this play' is incest or envy or the evils of usury; that goes to Jane Austen when – in a much more refined and delicate way – Lionel Trilling detects in her novels a deep understanding of the strengths and weaknesses of her society. And *Eugene Onegin* is at least as much like Jane Austen's novels as it is like *Tristram Shandy*.

There is an important sense, too, in which the aesthetic method – if it comes off – pre-empts such a critical response. This would be as true of Nabokov himself as it is of Pushkin and Gogol. The showman who dazzles us with his virtuosity and sleight of hand is also, and as a part of his skill, implying that the secret of his success is still hidden from us, that there is more behind this than meets the eye. With Gogol in particular the secret is an open secret – 'Gogol's secret' used to be a favourite concept of Russian critics – because there was to be a second part to *Dead Souls* that would reveal all and turn the strange negative fascination of the first part into something positive, pure, and uplifting. But, however hard he tried, the one trick that was not in the showman's power was to turn himself into the evangelist. Gogol burned his manuscript and died in despair when he realized that he could not be other than the showman genius he was; but the irony is that the implications of his masterpiece had already done all that an evangelist could do – indeed, much more, as is the way of true art – and made it unnecessary for him to try to be one.

The limitations of his magical power that drove Gogol to despair are not the limitations of decadence: they are just the opposite. The limitations of a decadent work are in some sense complacent, while those of a magician like Gogol disclose a haunted awareness of the worlds outside his own circle, 'the little blue flames of his humble hell', as Nabokov puts it. Nabokov's Humbert Humbert is, in his still more humble and more pathetic way, a kind of inspired variation on this very aspect of Gogol; and the most effective aspect of *Lolita* is the way in which the author appears (or affects) to be unaware of the implications of his own narrative, pushing them aside as a conjuror might do with props that spill out at an inopportune moment.

This is itself, we come to see, very much a part of the act. Lolita and her mother don't get on; but a realization of the unimportance of this hits the reader like cold water when Humbert lets him see the real situation in which he has contrived for his own ends – the ends of aesthetic bliss, of a sort – to place her. She is an orphan; she has no place to go. And it is this fact that looks out from behind all the devices of the book and the desires of its hero. The author places the sentence that reveals it with all the art with which Gogol leads up to one of his famous final sentences – 'Things are tedious in this world, gentlemen.' Nabokov quickly covers up the fact beneath the aesthetic clowning of the car journey, the shooting of Quilty; but it is still there. It keeps looking out, from beneath all Humbert's fantasies and all the conjuring tricks of the author, up to the scene in which a plain and pregnant Lolita is discovered married to her deaf war veteran. The fact confronts at every point the showmanship of the book, and art – real art, not 'aesthetic bliss' – is the beneficiary of the process.

Even more obviously than other novels of Nabokov *Lolita* is inspired by his enjoyment of Pushkin and Gogol. In his Gogol book he does the critical equivalent of the technique used creatively in *Lolita*. What about these dead souls? The 'point' of the story is that con-man and trickster Chichikov, 'neither fat nor thin, old nor young', the epitome of the contingent, has had the idea of buying up dead serfs from landowners. The landowners profit because they will not have to pay the property-tax levied on their notional roll of serfs between one census and another; while Chichikov can raise a mortgage on the serfs he will now officially possess.

Nabokov starts by vigorously belabouring the ludicrous idea of Gogol as a social satirist 'showing up' conditions in Russia. And, then, he slips in the following sentence: '*Morally* Chichikov was hardly guilty of any special crime in attempting to buy up dead men in a country where live men were lawfully purchased and pawned.' Well, exactly! The devastating fact, which sits calmly under Gogol's ingenious and spectacular fantasies, is something he doesn't even bother to mention; and Nabokov, more consciously deadpan, follows on. *Dead Souls* is exactly at the opposite end of the art-scale from *Uncle Tom's Cabin*, and yet, as Nabokov's sentence off-handedly admits, it is doing, by infinitely more fascinating means, the same job, and unmistakably conveying the same message.

Art has no job, insists Nabokov. Fine: only it just happens to be found to have done one – in *Lolita* no less than in *Dead Souls*. If Nabokov were not so deliberately combative, he would grant that, instead of insisting that there is only one proper end result – the purr of beatitude. For this is as absurd as saying that art gives us a message. In all great art the message is dissolved in the beatitude; we only know we have received it when we begin to realize how good the work is. Pushkin headed the fourth book of *Eugene Onegin* with a remark of Necker's, 'La morale est dans la nature des choses' – and he knew it was as much in the nature of art as it was in that of things in general.

Particularly of the vulgarity of things – all three writers are fascinated by that. The Russian word – less abstract and more comprehensive than vulgarity, more succulent in its powers of echoic suggestion – is *poshlost.* In his book on Gogol Nabokov gives us an idyll on the scope and shades of meaning embodied in this dumpy, sloshy word. In its particularly, though not peculiarly, Russian application, *poshlost* is the kind of vulgarity that buries facts behind gestures and pretences, settled phrases and habits of thought and speech. Chichikov, the hero of *Dead Souls*, is an embodiment of *poshlost*, which, then as now, cannot exist without turning the actual into the unreal, the low fact into the lofty cliché, the essential into the nothing in particular. In France, *poshlost* is everything that made Flaubert lick his lips over the project of writing a Dictionary of Received Ideas; in the Anglo-Saxon countries its most characteristic nest is in the world of films and advertising. A connoisseur of the American Dream, that totally *poshli* concept, Nabokov locates it in the magazine picture: 'A radio set (or a car or a refrigerator, or table silver – anything will do) has just come to the family: mother clasps her hands in dazed delight, the children crowd around, all agog ... even Grandma of the beaming wrinkles peeps out somewhere in the background (forgetful, we presume, of the terrific row she has had that very morning with her daughter-in-law); and somewhat apart ... stands triumphant Pop, the proud donor.' But this, as Nabokov notes, is a comparatively harmless and innocent *poshlost*, a conspiracy like that of the comics, which comforts many but deceives hardly anyone. In true *poshlost*, in 'powerful', 'moving' novels, for instance, the sham, as he says, is *not* obvious. At the same time, all human beings, in some degree, depend on it; and for that reason art does too, even the greatest. As artist and critic, Nabokov is fascinated by the relation of *poshlost* to art, and what art makes of it both by detaching itself and compromising itself.

Eugene Onegin provides many subtle and, at the same time, stylized examples of this process. Lensky, the poet and lover of Tatiana's sister Olga, is an absurd figure: both his love and his poetry make him absurd, though endearing; and if Eugene is a method in the poem, Lensky is to some extent its butt. But when he fights a duel with Eugene and is killed, all this changes; and the change is signalled in the two stanzas that describe his death. He dies encompassed by the sort of *poshli* images he himself might have used in his poems. He falls like snow detached by an avalanche and sliding down a mountain; his youthful bloom is withered, the flame on the altar extinguished. From the context these banalities acquire a touching, dreadful force, which is both reversed and confirmed in the next stanza by a simple image of, so to speak, Pushkin's own. 'The window panes have been chalked over; the lady of the house has gone, no one knows where.' By dying – 'the really distinguished thing' – Lensky has not only defeated his opponent but negated him. Lensky appears the true man, and Onegin the sham parody.

In Gogol's world *poshlost* has a more dubious relation to the effect. It is profoundly wearisome, boring, and depressing, and yet it may become comic, wonderful, witty. Gogol saturates his pages in it until the saturation itself becomes a marvellous feat of art. The denizens of the tale are equally bored by *poshlost* and dependent on it; the reader is simply enchanted by it. Thus, Chichikov, to take a minor instance, cannot talk to a young lady at a ball without bringing in 'some such topic as the vastness of the Russian Empire' – just as a middle-aged apparatchik today might bore a girl with rhapsodies about Soviet sputniks and submarines; and when the girl starts to yawn, he does not notice as he gains momentum and continues to tell her 'many pleasant things he has had occasion to relate before in similar circumstances, in various places',

namely, in Simbirsk province, at the house of Sofron Ivanovich Bezpechny, who had a daughter called Adelaida and three sisters-in-law; in Ryazan province, at Fedor Fedorovich Perekroev's; in Penza province, at Flor Vasilievich Pobedonosnoy's, and at Flor's brother's, Peter Vasilievich, with whom lived his sister-in-law Catherine and her second cousins Rose and Emily; in Vyatka province, at Peter Varsonofievich's, where resided the sister of his daughter-in-law, Pelageya Egorevna, and her niece Sophie, and her adopted sisters, one also Sophie, the other Maklatura.

'One also Sophie'.... Gogol knows that humanity lives in *poshlost* like a fish in water; and his art loves it and makes the most of it, while there is also despair in the fact that Chichikov, and all the rest of us, can only live in the little blue flames of our humble hell. Gogol's style, usually 'dishevelled' (Nabokov's word), soars into a special kind of grim rhapsody when he contemplates in *Dead Souls* what he sees as his task, a task that may one day become a sacred mission:

Happy is the writer who omits these dull and repulsive characters who disturb one by being so painfully real; who comes close to such that reveal the lofty nature of man; who from the great turmoil of images that whirl daily around him selects but a few exceptions ... who has never come down from those heights to visit his poor insignificant kinsmen, and remained aloof ... immersed in remote magnificent fancies ... those visions are a home and family to him, and at the same time the thunder of his fame rolls far and wide ... he is God.

But a different lot and another fate await the writer who has dared to evoke all such things as are constantly before one's eyes ... the shocking morass of trifles that has tied up our lives, and the essence of cold crumbling humdrum characters with whom our earthly way, now bitter, now dull, fairly swarms....

Quotation and translation are Nabokov's, who understands, as Gogol perhaps – it is an aspect of the greatness and the pathos of his art –

could not bring himself to do, that the visions that are a home and family to most people are of nymphets and new overcoats, like the one that is won and lost by Gogol's poor Akaky Akakyvich, and not of heaven and the saints. As Nabokov points out, Gogol's tragedy was that he was 'trying to write something that would please both Gogol the artist and Gogol the monk'. What he does not say is that Gogol was all the finer artist for wanting to be a monk. He loved the religious ideal as hopelessly as Akaky his overcoat, or Humbert his Lolita; and, if this is not human interest and the human sublime, what is? Humbert's infatuation puts him in the most *poshli* position possible; and Nabokov the author's not quite invisible sympathy does not entirely square with Nabokov the critic's amused contempt for 'human interest' and for those who seek it in literature. The point is to admit that we live in *poshlost*, and not to pretend (as the advertisement does) that *poshlost* is the highest happiness and the good life. Novels like Gogol's and Nabokov's tell the truth as the advertisement does not; and Tolstoy saw the end of art as to tell the truth. In short, it is the only way to Nabokov's purr of beatitude.

Nabokov was no doubt amused by the fact that his more sentimental female readers might secretly pine over Humbert as their predecessors did over Goethe's Werther; while some of his male ones might want to thrash the wretched Humbert within an inch of life for his conduct to the hapless nymphet. His hero Pushkin was aware of just the same double-take between authorial sympathy and detachment, and its relation to the client's own response. Shklovsky dryly pointed out that Pushkin parodies the traditional 'human interest' of the novel, and the sentiments it tries to arouse in our bosoms, to make us feel that he *really* loved and wept over his Tatiana, as he says he does. Nabokov might well talk about 'my Lolita' as Pushkin does about 'my Tatiana'. It may well be true that Pushkin's frequent assertions of love for his heroine, and of friendship and regard for his hero, are a way of conveying their wholly notional existence, their status as what he calls 'products of my fancy and of harmonious devices', a phrase that well describes how Nabokov himself sees his characters, and evidently thinks that we should see them.

By contrast, we cannot imagine Dostoevsky or Tolstoy – the first deprecated by Nabokov, the second admired but seldom referred to – talking about 'my Alyosha', 'my Natasha', or 'my Pierre'. The reason is plain. It is part of the authorial magician's patter to show affection for the puppets he is manipulating. But Dostoevsky and Tolstoy appear before us not as conjurors but as fellow-seekers, fellow-explorers of the questions, 'What's it about? How should one live?'; and so their characters are simply on a par with us and themselves. The weakness of Nabokov's position is that he regards this difference as fundamental, art being all on one side and mere 'human interest' on the other. No experienced reader could possibly agree with him. The methods may be different; but both lead us back to life in the end, as all good art does, including that of Nabokov himself. *Tristram Shandy* and *Eugene Onegin*, *Lolita* too, each has its way of making us confront life in all its fascinating unsatisfactoriness. Each contrives to make life appear *in* the magic, even if it is not of it. Slonimsky, a Pushkin scholar, truly observes that Tatiana's words to Onegin at the end of the novel – 'happiness was once so possible, so near' – echo through it with a strange resonance, as if what belonged to life could never be taken over by art.

The elegance of the poem is its comic negation – Tatiana falls for Onegin, and nothing comes of it; then he falls for her and nothing comes of that either – a tail-swallowing device like the single joke of *Tristram Shandy*. But happiness of the usual kind is somehow and somewhere present, perhaps in the tacit admission – a part of Pushkin's art – that Tatiana was created for the real world, and not, like Onegin, for that of the poem. Its mysterious but harmonious relation between the stringent pattern of art and the free, open queries about human life and human interest is more vital to its achievement than Nabokov will admit. But he is on safe ground when he points out the utter impossibility of Chichikov 'repenting', as his author desperately designed him to do, and ending his days as an emaciated monk in a Siberian monastery. 'No wonder that the author, in a last blinding flash of artistic truth, burnt the end of *Dead Souls*.' Certainly Chichikov could no more escape the *poshlost* of his existence, the little blue flames of his humble hell, than Humbert Humbert could have renounced *Lolita* or been a faithful husband to her mother, 'Big Haze'.

In practice, Nabokov treats Pushkin's poem, in his marvellous notes to it, as the great repository of 'human interest' that every reader has always found it. He lectures us in public, and with some justification, on our vulgar reading habits, but quietly accedes to them in private. Two instances are worth mentioning. Formalistically speaking, Onegin's 'trouble' is that he is only a character in a book, a kind of parody, as Tatiana begins to suspect when she looks at the marks he has made in the books of his own library. But Onegin, the eponymous hero and *point d'artifice* of the poem, comes very much alive when he realizes that he has killed Lensky, the butt of art because so naïvely committed to the *poshlost* of life. His remorse, though indicated with Pushkin's usual briefness, is as real as Macbeth's. It is a shock that drives him still further out of the living part of the poem: his final rejection by Tatiana does for him completely, and for the poem too, because it stops. Art has no choice but to surrender the floor to Life, which has no choice but to carry on in the ways it always does.

Nabokov does justice to the human side of Onegin's remorse; but he goes further. He breaks his own rule by suggesting that there is another and different kind of 'human interest' in the final rejection scene. Does Tatiana really mean it? She admits she loves Onegin – why deny it? – But she has married another and will remain true to him for life. Nabokov's scholarship, as exhaustive as it is unconventional, has worked over the many contemporary parallels for utterances of this kind. Is she uttering only a brisker Russian version of the words of Julie de Wolmar in her last letter to St Preux in Rousseau's novel *Emile*? There can be no doubt that Pushkin intended the decision to be a final one; 'but has he achieved his purpose?' For a hundred years ideological criticism has been devoted to 'passionately patriotic eulogies of Tatiana's virtue': Here is your frank, responsible, altruistic, heroic Russian woman. 'Actually the French, English and German women of Tatiana's favourite novels were quite as fervid and virtuous as she.' Nabokov always enjoys a dig at Russian and Soviet patriotism; but what he says shows us just how much Pushkin succeeded in having it both ways. He conflates an effective formalized ending with two kinds of 'human interest' ones. That splendid forthright Tatiana! How she gave Onegin what was coming to him! But perhaps she did not? Perhaps, life being what it is, she made her gesture, and then later on? ... Possibly much later on?

Nabokov's treacherous speculation is supported by the fact that Pushkin was at first reluctant to abandon his Onegin at the moment when art decreed he should cease to exist. Arm-in-arm with his hero – for Pushkin himself appears as a friend of Onegin in the poem – the author proposed to accompany him and the reader on a tour of Europe and the Middle East. But Onegin was no Don Juan; he had no relaxed co-existence with the consciousness of his creator, as had Byron's hero, a hero who could be kept going as long as the author had something fresh to write about. Pushkin wrote on for a while, but soon saw that the poem was over. His 'free novel', as he called it, to distinguish its particoloured tragi-comic pattern from the correctness of a classic form, had turned out to be, in another sense, not so free after all.

But, though the novel thus declared its proper shape and form for author and client reader alike, the client is not bound to act on the knowledge in the way the author was. *He* is free to follow up his own speculations; and it is part of the genius of the poem to invite him to do so. Nabokov points out that a singular property of *Eugene Onegin* is to confer amnesia on those most vociferous in praise of its 'representational' qualities. The invitation to treat it as a free novel is taken rather too much *au pied de la lettre*; and Dostoevsky – 'a much overrated, sentimental and Gothic novelist' – while praising Tatiana as a type of the 'positive Russian woman', labours under the singular delusion that 'her husband is a venerable old man', whereas he is in reality a sprightly and more successful near-contemporary of Onegin. Moreover, while pursuing his predetermined line that Tatiana is a true Russian, and Onegin a vagrant cosmopolitan, Dostoevsky affirms that the latter has wandered in foreign countries, a claim that the text and the historical period give him no warrant for at all. 'All of which goes to show that Dostoevsky had not really read *Evgeny* [*sic*] *Onegin*.'

Ah yes, but what is to read *Eugene Onegin*? Maybe Dostoevsky got his facts wrong; but, as traitor Nabokov cannot help insinuating, in the enchanted land of the poem facts remain agreeably debatable. Though we shall never know whether Tatiana really hardened her heart for ever against him, or whether Onegin went travelling or perhaps became a Decembrist revolutionary, such speculations not only enliven the poem still further, but even underpin its formal parabola. That purr of beatitude is really, as Nabokov knows quite well, a much more robust noise – the noise of continuing excitement, argument, debate.

Something of this fizzing freshness – exquisite art combined with what an orthodox artistic vocabulary cannot find the terms for – is to be found in Nabokov's version of Pushkin's verse novel. Its oddities, often seemingly perverse, have found few defenders; and it is often pointed out that Nabokov's outlandish vocabulary does not in the least resemble Pushkin's agile but always euphonious one. Pushkin is as melodious as he is decorous, his vocabulary always sprightly but never startling. In theory at least, although an imitation of the metre presents the translator with almost insuperable difficulties, it should not be so difficult to match in conventional English Pushkin's almost equally conventional poetic vocabulary. But in practice this is just where the various rhyming versions – with the exception of the most recent one, by Charles Johnston – most lamentably fall down.

What is lacking is the effervescent brio that Pushkin confers on his fairly unremarkable choice of words, making them seem wholly personal, idiosyncratically his own. It seems to me that the eccentric Nabokovian vocabulary is in its way an inspired correlative of this Pushkinian *brio*. Since Pushkin cannot be imitated, then let a completely literal version have its own parallel kind of individuality and high spirits. Nabokov's choice of the odd and sophisticated word that only he would have thought of provides a kind of intuitive and alternative centre, a creative counterpoint to Pushkin's inimitable distinction.

I make no apology for suggesting an explanation that Nabokov himself might have given if he had bothered, and if he had not been driven on to his high horse by the carping of the critics. It is important to note that his eccentric vocabulary never suggests *clumsiness* in the way that other translators' attempts to be sprightly invariably do. Nothing could be more disheartening, or merely grotesque, than the attempt to pursue Pushkinian *joie de vivre* in comic English. Babette Deutsch, for example, renders the arrival of Onegin in his last attempt on Tatiana in her Petersburg mansion as: 'Looking too corpselike to be nobby/He walks into the empty lobby' – a feat of infelicity almost as incomparable as the one translated from Tchaikovsky's admittedly already very inadequate libretto: 'I'm just a simple man of action/But I love Tatiana to distraction.' By contrast with this kind of thing the highly expressive exuberance of Nabokovisms ('Viatic lore', 'the shotman', 'the waists of his ripe daughters') might well, one feels, have appealed to the 'Attaboy' side of Pushkin himself.

As a translator and interpreter of some of the greatest, least accessible, and most misunderstood works in Russian literature, Nabokov has no equal. His own creative tastes and powers must take the credit for this, as well as his independence of all kinds of orthodox critical judgement and his stubborn refusal to make his theories seem more respectable, and more in keeping with the ideas about art and its functions that are current in our time. When the text needed it, he

Apparently the engagement of Nabokov's parents, who were married on 2 November 1897 (old style).

The house in Vyra, which was burned by the peasants after the Revolution. The rooms of Nabokov and his brother Sergey were on the top floor of the unseen side, as was the tutor's. The last windows on the right of the lower floor (of the sunlit façade) belong to the room where Nabokov kept his butterfly collection.

Opposite Nabokov's uncle on his mother's side, Vassily Rukavishnikov, around the turn of the century in the park of the Rozhestveno estate.

Top Bath-house on the Oredezh river in the old park of the Vyra estate.

Above Tennis on one of the three estates, c. 1900, with Nabokov's mother near right.

Nabokov's parents at the turn of the century on the Batovo estate.

Top On the Batovo estate around 1900: in front row *(second from left)* Nabokov's parental grandmother, Baroness Maria Korff; *(third from left)* Aunt Nata (Nathalie de Peterson), his father's eldest sister; *(fourth from left)* his mother Elena (née Rukavishnikov); *(fifth from left)* Aunt Bessy (Princess Elizaveta Sayn-Wittgenstein), another of his father's sisters; *(sixth from left)* his maternal grandmother, Olga Rukavishnikov. Behind stand all the village dignitaries.

Above Part of his Uncle Vasya's Rozhestveno estate – the main house is partially concealed by trees – as it appeared in 1969 from the Vyra side of the Oredezh river. The old wooden bridge, which is mentioned in *Speak, Memory*, has since been replaced. The village of Rozhestveno is visible on the left, and the bath-house that appears in illustration three is on the near side of the river, to the left. The Vyra estate and the ancient cemetery are behind the observer, along an uphill road. The Batovo estate is two versts to the right.

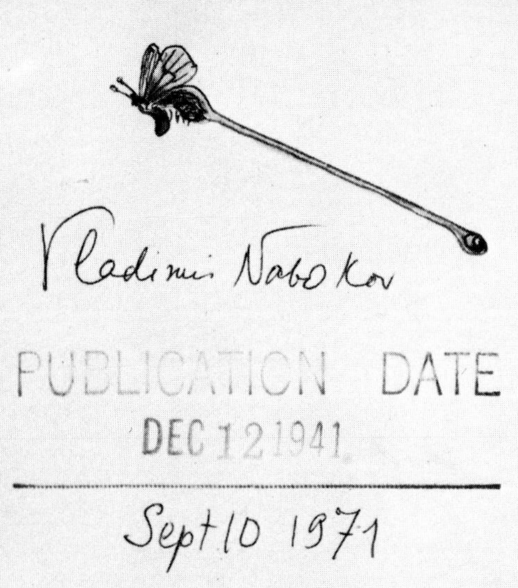

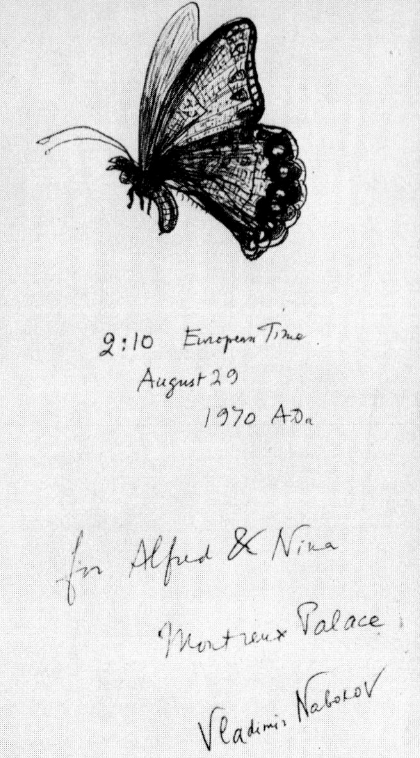

Left 'I obtained my first Nabokov book, the out-of-print *Real Life of Sebastian Knight*, at the Gotham Book Mart in New York City in 1953 for $3.50 – the same price as any common new novel. Sans dust jacket, a vulnerable and friendless review copy whose flyleaf bore the large and rude imprint "PUBLICATION DATE/Dec 12 1941", the dusty and faded book looked as though it had been on its obscure shelf since that date, possibly a victim of Pearl Harbor, certainly a symbolic object, proffering another hidden but not so secret message: *who is Nabokov*? Almost twenty years later, when Nabokov was established securely and visibly as Nabokov, I asked him to inscribe my sentimental edition of *Sebastian Knight*. He did so (in six or seven colours), balancing and arranging his drawn butterfly, signature and dateline in such a way that the unsightly publication notice took on the elegance and logic of design of one of those Saul Steinberg caprices in line which at once incorporate, contemplate, transform, and combat the gummed labels or rubber-stamped seals and imprinted injunctions of our commercial and bureaucratic civilization.' (Alfred Appel Jnr)

Above right 'As a youth in St Petersburg, Nabokov received expert training from the drawing masters who came to the house from 1907 until 1914. Of these tutors, M. V. Dobuzhinsky was the best known. "He made me depict from memory, in the greatest possible detail, objects I had certainly seen thousands of times without visualizing them properly: a street lamp, a postbox, the tulip design on the stained glass of our front door. He tried to teach me to find the geometrical co-ordinations between the slender twigs of a leafless boulevard tree, a system of visual give-and-takes, requiring a precision of linear expression, which I failed to achieve in my youth, but applied gratefully, in my adult instar, not only to the drawing of butterfly genitalia during my seven years at the Harvard Museum of Comparative Zoology, when immersing myself in the bright wellhole of a microscope to record in Indian ink this or that new

structure; but also, perhaps, to certain *camera-lucida* needs of literary composition." When I asked Nabokov to inscribe our copy of *Ada*, he demonstrated that Dobuzhinsky's lessons had indeed been applied, in the fullest sense. Using a handy ballpoint pen rather than his customary coloured pencils, he made a spare and elegant line drawing of a butterfly, starkly marking the venation of the wings, then signed it with an appropriate mock-exactitude (*Ada*'s Van Veen contemplates the texture of time), punningly dated it ("1970 ADa"), and was about to return the book when he had second thoughts and began to enhance the wings: for ten more minutes he shaded and stippled the butterfly, clearly having fun ("a rare species and a unique specimen, absolutely unique!") yet working with the kind of fierce concentration he must have brought to his index cards, these small units of space on which he tried to describe his – cosmos?' (Alfred Appel Jnr)

Above left 'This "manly specimen" (as Nabokov enigmatically called it) of a "Japanese species" (is this true?) was drawn and inscribed in lead pencil and red pen, as the broadly punning place-name may suggest. Nabokov's dozen or so inscriptions for us inevitably include a butterfly, with the exception of the Russian émigré first and only edition of *Mary* (*Mashenka*, 1926), which offers drawings of "egg", "larva", and "pupa" – as befits an immature first novel, its metamorphosis forever incomplete.' (Alfred Appel Jnr)

Above right 'Special effects by VN Productions in my copy of the émigré edition of *Camera Obscura*, created in seven colours forty years after its publication. It is Nabokov's most "cinematic" novel, and the larger butterfly suggests that he might have had a brilliant career as a movie publicist, inasmuch as the Cyrillic lettering on its wing proclaims the name of book and author, a promotional gimmick that is not utilized often enough.' (Alfred Appel Jnr)

'Vladimir Nabokov "at home", Ithaca, N.Y., 1958, shortly before "Hurricane Lolita/Swept from Florida to Maine" (*Pale Fire*), allowing him – at sixty – to resign his professorship and write full-time. My qualifying quotation marks are by way of stating that exile Nabokov was never at home, literally or figuratively, after his departure from Russia in 1919. Never again would he own a residence. With Beckett he was our laureate of the lonely room, the saddest of digs. During their decade at Cornell the Nabokovs moved each year, sometimes every semester, renting the apartments or houses of professors who were on leave from the university. Often enough the contents of these domiciles offered the novelist source material, knicknacks to help fill Charlotte Haze's living room or the titles of old best-sellers to place on a shelf in one of Pnin's drafty rented rooms. A Cornell professor, now retired, recalls how the Nabokovs visited him as potential tenants in the early 1950s. He and his wife set out to show their visitors the house, a boring tour for all concerned. They walked down the hall and, at their initial stop, the professor dutifully opened the door to the room of his two young daughters, who were out playing. "Darling!" said Nabokov, calling to his wife, already a straggler. "Come here! Look at this charming furniture,"

and he pointed to a small, scaled-down table and three chairs, the appropriate toy china, silverware, and tiny napkins neatly set for that afternoon's tea. "We'll take it!" announced Nabokov, though they had not yet inspected the plumbing or master bedroom. Good readers and casual film-goers may recall an analogous moment in *Lolita* when Humbert the room-seeker first tours the Haze home. Is it intolerably academic to ponder Nabokov's impulsive decision? Had the children's room sounded some plangent chord of nostalgia? Evoked his beloved *Alice in Wonderland* (which he had translated into Russian)? Personified *Homo ludens*, irresistibly? Signalled, in its sweet perfection, its cosiness, that All Goes Well within *this* house? Or had the novelist-naturalist spied some quotidian details which called for unhurried scrutiny before he could utilize them in Humbert's field guide to American girl children? And, aside from being an allusion to Lewis Carroll, did the cat in the photograph belong to Nabokov? No, he told me it came with the house. "No pets," he said, solemnly. "Nor nymphets," he added, for posterity.' (Alfred Appel Jnr. Photo by Maclean Dameron)

Above Nabokov and Alfred Appel Jnr a few minutes after the incident described on page 27.

Nabokov's lectern in his Montreux apartment.

Vladimir Nabokov in Montreux.

Armed with his butterfly net and cigarettes, Nabokov pauses during a walk with his son Dmitri on La Videmanette, a mountain at Rougemont, near Gstaad.

could be a sober and self-effacing translator. There is little to be said about his version of Lermontov's *A Hero of our Time*, and his introduction to it, except that they are wholly adequate and informative, perfectly suited to the work and its author. But about Pushkin and Gogol Nabokov is very much more than that. Pushkin himself scribbled on one of the margins of the *Eugene Onegin* manuscript the comment that 'translators are the post-horses of civilization'. Nabokov knows what civilization is about; and, when he brings Pushkin and Gogol to us, he shows us just how civilized, how sophisticated, how radiantly cosmopolitan, their wonderful Russian masterpieces are.

To find this out, and to begin our education in them, it is necessary to do no more than to read the description of the garden of old Plyushkin, the miser in *Dead Souls*, which Nabokov translates for us in his little book on Gogol. He prefaces it with a few remarks on the sense of colour in prose description: 'Before his and Pushkin's advent Russian literature was purblind.... The sky was blue, the dawn red, the foliage green, the eyes of beauty black, and so on. It was Gogol (and after him Lermontov and Tolstoy) who first saw yellow and violet at all.' In the Lermontov Introduction he notices that 'lilac' is used for the first time as a colour adjective in Russian literature, and how unassumingly it slips into place in the spare prose of *A Hero of our Time.* I think it may be misleading of him to mention Pushkin in this context, for Pushkin's vocabulary was as colloquial but also as conventional as Byron's; and we may remember that it was Byron who ridiculed Coleridge's description of the evening sky 'with its peculiar tint of yellow green'. But Nabokov has surely hit on just the right analogy when he says that 'the description of Plyushkin's garden shocked Russian readers in much the same way as Manet did the bewhiskered philistines of his day.'

At the same time, there is a great deal more than a new kind of description in the passage that Nabokov gives from *Dead Souls.* The complexity of poetry and feeling in them is a revelation, a revelation of the way in which the most sophisticated observation of a scene, and the simplest, most fervent response to it, co-exist in this more than magical prose. It makes such a text as *The Waves* (which Virginia Woolf also thought of as a poem) look like mere fine writing, the produce of a Silver Age. That Russian epoch to which Nabokov acts as our mentor and guide was truly Golden. He knows it, and shows it to be so: the fact that he affects to recommend to us concepts of approval more suited to decadent or Silver-Age writing only makes this more clear, the expression of his contempt for critics whose reverence for the 'classics' is, in fact, a way of using them, for their own purposes or that of the current ideological fashion. The 'purr of beatitude' is his recipe for blocking off all those gentry, and propelling us to the most direct and most delighted response to the text.

5 Nabokov's Uses of Pattern

Alex de Jonge

'Philosophically I am an indivisible monist,' Nabokov once observed. The indivisible monist who would also write novels is faced with a very particular problem. In the nineteenth century the novel was the supreme form for the reflection of change, decline, dispersion. 'The form of absolute sinfulness', as Fichte termed it, it was the medium that captured the very texture of a meaningless existence which simply took place in time, unstructured by any pattern of transcendent meaning. Time was the only value that it acknowledged, and time was shown to triumph over all forms of human aspiration – the supreme example being Flaubert's *Education Sentimentale*, which simply traced the journey of its hero down the river of time towards death, reminding us that beyond the texture of haphazard day-to-day existence there was nothing – except for the knowledge that such experience was all there was.

As we shall see, nothing could be further from Nabokov's stance than this kind of nihilism, reflected in the remorseless linearity of Flaubert's novel. This gives the impression that it is being created through and in the course of the aimless day-to-day experience of its central character. The novels of Nabokov, on the other hand, may be said to pre-exist their characters. They are already there *à l'état virtuel* before they are written. 'The design of my novel is fixed in my imagination, and every character follows the course I imagine for him. I am the perfect dictator in that private world in so far as I alone am responsible for its stability and truth.' One of those characters, Fedor Godunov-Cherdyntsev in *The Gift*, displays an identical attitude to the design of chess problems: 'If he had not been certain, as he also was in the case of literary creation, that the realization of the scheme already existed in some other world, from which he transferred it into this one [the work would have been an impossible burden] since it would have to concede ... the possibility of its impossibility.'

This attitude is quite central to Nabokov's techniques of fiction, and, indeed, to his conception of the ultimate significance of fiction, one that goes a little way beyond pure aesthetics. It is reflected in his novels in a number of ways, of which the most important and most enduring is his concern that his novels should be patterned. He makes his novels function on two frequently interpenetrating levels: the level of the 'reality' they depict and that created by the way in which that depiction is organized. This second level will take on an increasing importance for Nabokov, and is most evident in the way in which he imposes artificial authorial patterns, overloading his works with obvious contrivance and coincidence.

This practice finds its first and admittedly modest expression in *Mary*, where it is based on a somewhat superficial interplay between space and time. The action opens on Sunday, 1 April 1924. Mary is due to arrive from Russia six days later, on Saturday, 7 April, the morning of Ganin's departure from Berlin. Throughout the book the author is careful to remind us what day of the week we have arrived at. The 'spatial' dimension provides a contrived complement to that first week in April. The *pension* consists of six rooms facing one another across a corridor. The somewhat hopeless landlady has labelled them with leaves from a calendar for 1923 – the first week of April. In the course of six days Ganin enters each one of the rooms for a particular scene; and, when there are no more days – or rooms – left, he abandons both the *pension* and the book, setting off for France. It is an admittedly modest pattern, in a modest novel, but introduces a technique that he made much more elaborate use of in the books to come.

For all the sophistication of their narratives, the early novels do not, on the whole, take this pattern-making much beyond the setting up of networks of repetition and coincidence which remind us that these fictions are not mere slices of life: they are ordered; and we are frequently afforded glimpses of 'the puppeteer's giant hand' doing the ordering. This emerges, for example, in the following passage: 'That little trip to Pomerania Bay was in fact proving quite a boon for everyone concerned, including the god of chance (Cazelty or Sluch or whatever his real name was), once you imagined that god in the role of a novelist or playwright, as Goldemar had in his most famous work.'

The work in question is entitled *King, Queen, Knave*. The apparent coincidences that form the patterns of this book are the work of a novelist's fate, practising practical jokes at the expense of his characters and gratifying his sense of black humour. He makes them walk through a predetermined pattern whereby a would-be murderer, Martha, who hopes her husband has a weak heart, may get influenza or will drown, herself has a bad heart and dies of influenza which she catches on a boat trip, while the husband remains obstinately alive.

Glory makes more elaborate use of pattern and repetition. Martin Edelweiss, one of Nabokov's most agreeable heroes, is a young man whose dreams literally come true. A train journey he makes to the South of France, for example, shortly before his final exploit, is the repetition and elaboration of a journey he made to Biarritz with his family before the war. But Martin does more than re-enact the past. He follows a destiny determined long before his birth. In his nursery there used to hang a picture of a Russian forest painted by his grandmother, *née* Indrikov. The *indrik* was a legendary animal of Russian folklore, 'King of all the beasts'; and with that name Nabokov conjures up quintessential Russian magic and the marvellous beasts that left their spoor on unknown paths in Pushkin's dreamy introduction to *Ruslan and Lyudmilla.*

The picture shows a path winding through the forest. In childhood Martin had associated it with the story of an English boy who had a similar picture in his bedroom; one day he entered it to disappear into the woods. This is what Martin feels he will do when he sets off on his journey back to Russia. The novel ends with an English friend, Darwin, who has been to see Martin's mother, leaving a wood by a forest path, walking out of the picture into which Martin had returned, never to reappear, creating 'a furious finale although nothing much happens at the very end – just a bird perching on a wicket in the greyness of a wet day'.

Besides patterns such as this, which stand at the very centre of a novel, Nabokov can provide secondary embellishments, echoing repetitions that have no function other than to signal that the work is indeed patterned. Witness two minor motifs in *Despair.* One is the colour lilac. Hermann sees his imaginary mother as a languid lady in lilac silks. The wrappers of the chocolates he manufactures have a woman in lilac on them. A public garden in the town where he meets Felix, his would-be double, has lilac bushes in it. He wears a lilac tie at this and a subsequent meeting, and, when preparing to commit murder, puts on his favourite lilac tie. A second pattern is created with the recurrence of the number nine. He gets the letters Felix writes to him from window No. 9 at the post office. He first writes to him on 9 March, and kills him on 9 March in Chapter 9. There is no special significance attached to this kind of patterning; it simply reminds us that we are placed in a designed and aesthetically controlled universe of Nabokov's own making.

We find the first really elaborate use of pattern in *The Defence*, a work that can only be read properly if its patterns are properly perceived – properly, because Nabokov has laid a trap for superficial readers. His introduction draws our attention to the numerous check-tiled floors, patterns of light and shade, gardens laid out like chessboards that stud the book, as Luzhin plays imaginary games of chess between light and shade. Yet there is a second, subtler pattern, its repetitions less obvious and much more dangerous, which is responsible for provoking Luzhin's ultimately suicidal defence. Luzhin, it will be recalled, had a breakdown in the course of a game of chess with his arch rival Turati. He has been told he must never play again. The pattern begins when Luzhin, dazed and in a Berlin flat, believes that he has returned to Russia. He is diverted by the dream, which he regards, in chess terms, as the witty repetition of a certain combination; but there is much more to it than that. It is the beginning of a whole series of such repetitions which will send him mad. From the moment of his collapse the rest of his life will consist of the echoing re-enactment of past events which builds up to a second and final breakdown. The latter part of the book can only be understood when it is seen as the delicate echoing of Luzhin's past, with subtle variations. Gradually Luzhin becomes aware that he is in a game played by 'the chess gods', and that they are developing some dreadful combination against him which he cannot anticipate. Eventually, as the pressure mounts up, he finds the key to the combination. He meets his one-time manager and evil genius Valentinov, who proposes that Luzhin act himself in a film; the object of the combination has been to lure him back into the game that almost destroyed him: 'By an implacable repetition of moves it was leading once more to that same passion which would destroy the dream of life.' Luzhin is convinced that the only way to avoid defeat is to make the ultimate sacrifice and leave the game. He attempts to by climbing through a hole in the board – a frosted glass window – into the black beyond. But Luzhin can never leave the game. As he falls, 'the whole black chasm was seen to divide into dark and pale squares, and Luzhin saw exactly what kind of eternity was obligingly and inexorably spread out before him'.

Luzhin is remarkable among Nabokov's characters for his capacity to perceive the patterns that inform his life, for, as Nabokov wrote in *Bend Sinister*, 'As with so many phenomena of time, recurrent combinations are perceptible as such only when they cannot affect us any more.' Perhaps it is as well, for perception of naked pattern places the sanity at risk. Adam Krug finds his philosophical speculations lead him to the digging of a pit that contains 'pure smiling madness'. Another character, Falter, in *Ultima Thule*, succeeds quite by chance in apprehending the universe 'as it really is', cracking the codes of consciousness and discovering the secret of secrets. He goes out of his mind for some time before making a partial recovery. He once told the secret to someone else, who promptly committed suicide.

Increasingly one has to be aware of the role Nabokov's often delicate and scarcely perceptible patterns play in his books if one is to hope to make a full reading of them. Thus, early in *The Real Life of Sebastian Knight* we come across a list of books in Knight's library. The narrator detects a strange melody in the list; and so he should. The books, more or less in the order in which they are arranged, will have a series of echoes in the course of the work to come: some featuring in descriptions of Knight's novels, others in the main narrative, helping to bring about that interpenetration of the two which is the whole point of that work. Thus, we find an echo of *Hamlet*, the first title on the shelf, in Knight's first novel, about a fat student who comes home to find his mother married to his uncle, an ear specialist, who has poisoned his father. Much of the echoing is a great deal subtler than this; and there are moments when the melody almost dies away, until it is finally rounded off with *King Lear*, the final title, since the death of a king, or checkmate, is a proper conclusion to a book that abounds in references to chess.

Echoing of this kind is much more than a gratuitous virtuosity. It is vital to Nabokov's conception of the form of fiction, of the novel as a self-reflecting form, circular rather than linear, constituting its own autonomous and self-justifying world. The hero of *The Gift*, Fedor Godunov-Cherdyntsev, aspires to this kind of narrative form with his *Life of Chernyshevsky*, 'a spiral within a sonnet', which opens with the tercets of the sonnet in question and concludes with its opening quatrains, so that the beginning of the sonnet sends us back to the beginning of the biography in order to complete it with the tercets; and round we go again.

The Gift itself is informed by a more elaborate circularity still, one that recalls Proust. Both *A la Recherche* and *The Gift* are about the making of a novelist. Both close their circles by leaving us at the point at which the central character is about to write the novel we have just read. When, at the end of the book, Fedor tells Zina his idea for a novel, the story of fate's various efforts at uniting them, his observation illuminates the book we have just read. It is only in the light of Fedor's intentions that we can now understand the importance of what have hitherto appeared trivial episodes. He, and we, achieve a fuller understanding of fate's mysterious patterns – even though Fedor is not aware of fate's final irony, since the two lovers-to-be have successfully locked themselves out of their flat.

As usual the character's apprehension of the pattern informing his life is a partial one. Fedor does not seem to realize that the last chapter of the book consists of a highly compressed reworking of the whole set of events that had taken place hitherto, in a whole series of almost imperceptible echoes. *The Gift* opens with the poet inventing a non-existent review of his poems. He then visits some friends named Chernyshevsky, where it is facetiously suggested he write the life of their famous namesake. We then hear of the death of Chernyshevsky *fils*. On his return Fedor is nearly locked out of his flat. He attends an absurd play-reading and has an imaginary conversation with another poet. He then makes contact with his mother, who talks to him about his sister's marriage; and this leads him to work on the life of his father, an episode culminating in his recollection of a walk through the streets of Petrograd to learn of his father's probable death.

The final chapter opens with real reviews of his book on Chernyshevsky. We then learn of the death of Chernyshevsky *père*. Most of the guests at the original soirée appear at the funeral. Next comes a literary meeting that echoes the play-reading; and, shortly after, Fedor goes for a walk near the spot where the young Chernyshevsky committed suicide. The lock-out theme is repeated when he has to go home in a bathing-suit since someone has stolen his clothes. He writes a long letter to his mother, saying how happy he is that his sister has had a child. Then, one night, he gets a midnight call to his old lodgings; walking through the streets as he once walked through Petrograd, he sees in a shop, looking at an atlas, the man who had called on him in Petrograd, asking him to come and see his uncle, the geographer, who gave him news of his father. He reaches his lodgings and has a blissful reunion with his parents. Although this turns out to be a dream, he finds in the circularity and repetition an ultimate assurance that 'everything was all right and simple, that this was the true resurrection, that it could not be otherwise'. In other words, the very fact of these repetitions, on the level of 'dream' or 'reality', is itself a kind of salvation, the demonstration that the world is ordered, planned and meaningful, not random and haphazard.

For there is much more to Nabokov's conception of pattern than pure aesthetics, narrative strategy; and it is *The Gift* that first offers any comment on the wider ramifications of Nabokov's sense of pattern. This book makes it clear that pattern is found not just in art, but also in nature; the matching or mis-matching of pattern is a characteristic of nature herself, and it is this that explains Nabokov's passion for entomology. Just as the echoes and repetitions that Fedor found in the life of Chernyshevsky 'pleased the gamester in the historian', it pleases the gamester in the naturalist to observe the patterns of nature, 'that exquisite cheat'. The disguises, echoes and imitations of imitations to be found in butterflies 'seem to have been invented by some waggish artist precisely for the intelligent eyes of man'. It is as the supreme source of pattern and seeming coincidence that nature fascinates Nabokov, and stimulates his own creative strategies. Her ingenious deceptions are described as 'bewitchingly divine'; and the Russian word for divine, *bozhestvenno*, is much stronger than its English equivalent, having none of its *mondain* overtones. Nabokov once observed that he would not have said the little he has about God had he not had a great deal more to say. *The Gift* introduces a notion that Nabokov never more than hints at, that there is no pattern without a pattern-maker. He hints at the possibility of an infinitely sophisticated version of the argument from design; and this, in turn, is associated with the idea of the human consciousness as a restrictive prison ('Down, Plato, down, good dog') that prevents us from perceiving things as they really are.

It is through the perception of pattern and the subtle echoes of apparent coincidence that one may gain an occasional glimpse of 'the truth'. The ability to perceive patterns is a vital aspect of the artist's gift, which gives him a sense of an unspecified something just beyond his normal powers of perception. Fedor has it to some extent. 'Fedor suddenly felt . . . the strangeness of life, the strangeness of its magic, as if a corner of it had been turned back for an instant and he had glimpsed its unusual lining,' while this kind of sensitivity stands in contrast to the philistine's capacity to 'misread' pattern. As Chernyshevsky senior lies dying, he observes that he knows there is no after-life as clearly as he knows it is raining – as he listens to someone in the flat above watering his window-boxes.

The Gift, then, is Nabokov's first full treatment of a view of the world as a kind of metaphysical chess problem, to which there is a key, a key to be found by a proper examination of the pieces on the board – as opposed to searching beyond the board itself. As his invented author Delalande observes: 'We are not going anywhere, we are sitting at home, the other world surrounds us always and is not at all at the end of some pilgrimage. In our earthly house windows are replaced by mirrors; the door, until a given time, is closed, but air comes in through the cracks.' The world contains a secret that our inadequate, 'stay at home senses' are scarcely capable of cracking, although sometimes, for an instant, they catch a corner turned back. It is this view of the secret, which may reveal aspects of itself through the quirks of pattern and design, that is finally responsible, not just for the form of Nabokov's novels, for his interest in butterflies, but for his very conception of the nature of art and the art of nature.

Read in ignorance of his earlier work, *Pale Fire* might appear to be a mere exercise in narrative pyrotechnics; and it certainly contains enough of them to engage the interest of determined exegetists; but, considered in the light of Nabokov's enduring concerns with pattern, the limitations of consciousness and the argument from design, it takes on a much richer charge of meaning to become one of his most complete examinations of these topics. Kinbote's commentary on Shade's poem creates the most extraordinary exercise in the matching, or mis-matching, of pattern. There is no better instance of the author's love of 'the confusion of two realities'. Yet, despite the apparent aberrations of the commentary, Shade and Kinbote have much in common; they share a common interest in 'the secret' and a desire to reach beyond the prisons of their consciousness. Moreover, Shade is indeed murdered; and aspects of both his life and his death form part of a great pattern, the weave of which we occasionally glimpse throughout the book. Shade shares Nabokov's own concern with prisons and patterns, wishing to reach out beyond the limitations of 'the painted cage' in which he finds himself. One such attempt was occasioned by a vision of a fountain he saw when nearly dying of a heart attack. He reads in a paper of a woman who had an identical vision, and visits her only to learn that there was a misprint in the paper and that, in fact, it was a mountain that she saw. This brings him to a conclusion that is vital to the understanding of the role of quirky pattern and seeming coincidence both here and elsewhere in Nabokov's work:

> Life Everlasting-based on a misprint!
> I mused as I drove homeward: take the hint,
> And stop investigating my abyss?
> But all at once it dawned on me that *this*
> Was the real point, the contrapuntal theme;
> Just this: not text, but texture; not the dream
> But topsy-turvical coincidence,
> Yes! It sufficed that I in life could find
> Some kind of link-and-boblink, some kind
> Of correlated pattern in the game,
> Plexed artistry, and something of the same
> Pleasure in it as they who played it found.

The lines could stand as the ultimate expression of Nabokov's own fascination with pattern and coincidence. Pattern is meaningful in itself because it is the opposite of random and chaotic chance. The very idea of coincidence is a contradiction in terms and evidence of a designer's hand. *Pale Fire* is founded in coincidence, the work of a 'combinational fate'. An American poet, John Shade, has as a temporary neighbour a Russian, V. Botkin, who is mad. Botkin believes himself to be the ex-King of Zembla, and tries to impose Zemblan material upon the poem Shade is writing. Shade has all but finished it when a second lunatic, Jack Grey, arrives, mistakes Shade for the judge who sentenced him, and shoots, while Botkin advances to draw his fire, taking him for a Zemblan assassin sent out to despatch King Charles. Whatever conjunction combinational fate set out to achieve, several mistakes have been made, since, as Shade himself once pointed out, different people see different similarities and similar differences. Nature, the grand cheat, has arranged various sets of elements – an unfinished poem, an émigré's fantasy, an escaped lunatic – and brought them together into a particular and quite deadly pattern, so quietly that, as they lock into place, one cannot even hear them click. In other words, the elements of *Pale Fire* constitute precisely that kind of topsy-turvical pattern that Shade has learnt to look for. Shade's poem and Nabokov's book are both celebrations of pattern as evidence of some kind of transcendental order, or at least some kind of 'supernal game'.

Yet it would be wrong to ascribe to Nabokov anything as simple as a modern version of the benign deism of the eighteenth century as exemplified by Pope, despite the many references to *The Essay on Man* to be found in *Pale Fire.* Nabokov is both delicate and tentative in his presentation of pattern. Moreover, he is a novelist, not a metaphysician; and it is an essential characteristic of novels that they question and challenge the propositions they advance through irony and ambiguity. The very fact that he makes such ample use of flawed or deranged characters suggests that the insights they arrive at are open to question. Perhaps, rather than affirm through his fictions that the world is ordered and patterned, he interrogates it in the hope that it might be. Order is more an aspiration than an article of faith; and, even if there is such order, it is by no means certain that it is benign. There may indeed be a supernal game; but the players are not necessarily benevolent. Nabokovian characters, caught in games, frequently have their wings torn off before they are killed for sport. Witness the wretched fate of Albinus in *Laughter in the Dark*, for example. The book introduces the notion of fate as a malign prankster via the musings of Axel Rex: 'The stage manager whom Rex had in view was an elusive double triple self-reflecting magic Proteus or a phantom, the shadow of many coloured glass balls flying in a curve, the ghost of a juggler on a shimmering curtain.'

It is *Lolita* that provides us with the most complete examination of Rex's Proteus, as Humbert Humbert becomes slowly aware that he is, like Luzhin, enmeshed in a pattern that he can sense, but not unravel. Thus he felt instinctively on his second journey with Lolita that telephone kiosks and lavatories were 'points at which my destiny was liable to catch', as Lolita would make contact with an as yet invisible presence. Similarly, he finds Lolita's illness just before she disappears part of a theme with the same taste and tone as a series of linked impressions that had puzzled and tormented him throughout the journey. Like Luzhin, Humbert is caught in a pattern of nightmare, as a superior force, in the first instance Quilty, regulates his life, shaping a journey he believes to be as random as the first trip, but that has been planned long before.

Humbert eventually finds the key to the pattern when Lolita names Quilty and he destroys him. He then builds into his memoir the whole network of clues and portents that might have led him to Quilty, as they might lead us while we read. Once his identity is revealed, the pattern locks into place, becomes clearly discernible, where a moment before it was a scrambled confusion. 'Quietly the fusion took place, and everything fell into order, into the pattern of branches I have woven through this memoir with the express purpose of having the ripe fruit fall at the right moment.'

Although Quilty is immediately responsible for the pattern that enmeshes Humbert, he is only the minion of a greater prankster yet, 'McFate' himself. It is McFate who set up the whole game; and McFate is something quite close to the devil. Nymphets, we are told, are demonic figures. Lolita would have driven Humbert mad with frustration, 'had not the devil realized that I was to be granted some relief if he wanted to have me as a plaything for much longer'. It is McFate who arranges Charlotte Haze's accident – 'precise fate, that synchronising phantom'. Humbert, in his attempts to keep Lolita, realizes that he is fighting fate itself; and we see him unsuccessfully trying to 'catch her elbow, and, I added, to change the direction of fate, Oh God, Oh God'. Although Humbert may feel that the whole pattern has fallen into place with the revelation of Quilty's identity, that was only a part of a greater pattern still, one that uses every character in the book to play a supernal game for the delectation of McFate – who does not feel responsible for any inconvenience suffered by its players.

In his last two novels Nabokov sustains his concern with the implications of pattern, notably in *Transparent Things*, where he brings a great delicacy to his treatment of the topic. The story of Person's three visits to Switzerland, his courtship and unwitting killing of his wife Armande, and his subsequent burning to death in the Ascot hotel, makes for a slight, sad book that reeks of death, but also suggests that death is a mere rite of passage from our world into an ampler one in which things have become transparent. The narrator, who is privileged with this sense of transparency, has achieved a supernatural degree of insight and vision that gives him a measure of control over Person, to the point of occasionally attempting to give him a push in the right direction. This is a far cry from the ostentatious puppet-master of earlier novels, a view of authorial providence that is infinitely gentler and more sophisticated. The nature of the narrative voice is not made too clear by Nabokov. It may be divine, providential or merely authorial; suffice it to say that it establishes a higher level of being and consciousness, one that transcends Person, that sees the past and has views about the relative probability of future events. It is a level to which Person apparently transfers through death.

The pattern regulating *Transparent Things* has two branches, murder and fire. Early in the book Person notices a green model of a skier in a shop. It was carved in jail by a homosexual convict, Armand Rave, who has strangled his boyfriend's incestuous sister, anticipating Person's strangling of Armande, who used to ski in green. On his final visit Person buys the statuette, which is in his room when he burns to death. The fire pattern is more elaborate. It is first found in the plot of one of Mr R.'s novels; a girl sets fire to a doll's house and burns a villa down. The book has flames on the cover. Armande is afraid of fires in hotels. She decided that a certain hotel in Stresa looked combustible, and that the last night of a stay in a hotel is statistically the most dangerous. She requires Person to indulge in some lunatic fire practice, clambering down the outside of their room. This anticipates his killing her in his sleep as he dreams he is carrying a girl to safety from a burning hotel-room. The fire that kills Person is the direct echo of that dream fire, combining the two themes of fire and murder. Their node, or meeting-place, is a seemingly casual quotation. An entry in Person's diary meditates on his blend of talent and clumsiness. He can draw landscapes, but cannot portray panic in the blazing windows of a villa. When he speaks French, he cannot lose his Canadian accent as he whispers 'Ouvre ta robe Déjanire that I may mount sur mon bûcher.' The reference is anticipatory and crucial. Déjanire sent Hercules the Nessus shirt to win back his love. The pain was so great that he burnt himself on a pyre. When he is about to be burnt, Person dreams that Armande is coming back to him. Instead, it is the fire that destroys him and wins him back. The phrase associates this with an act of self-immolation and hints that Armande is indirectly responsible for it.

The narrative voice goes on to suggest that Person's pilgrimage in search of the dead Armande is vain. *The Gift* told us that the other world surrounds us always, and is not at the end of some pilgrimage. The real interest of the book now begins to emerge. It is a tale of Person and the other world. Person, on his death, and like Bunyan's Mr Christian, a progressing pilgrim of a different sort, will cross over to some other side. Pattern and coincidence once again suggest a degree of providential order in 'the whole sorry business'.

Mr R., the author, is also concerned with death. In his last, and moving, letter to his publisher he regrets that he cannot render death, not being able to 'express in one flash what can only be understood immediately'. Yet this is what Nabokov sets out to do with the death of Person. The passage describing the flames dancing into his room is one of his finest, as they hold up delicate hands to prevent him leaving. Yet they also assist his exit. The last vision Person has is a view of the prison of conciousness. The narrative voice had earlier described life as a series of vegetables from a first picture book, spinning round a dreaming boy to form a ring of colours around a dead person or planet. This is what the dying Person sees, the colours reminding him of a childhood picture of triumphant vegetables spinning round a boy who tries desperately to awake from his dream – which is what Person does awakening from the nightmare of life. Death is not mere crude anguish; it is escape: 'The incomparable pangs of the mysterious mental manoeuvres needed to pass from one state of being to another.' The book ends with the words of a benevolent Mr R. welcoming Person aboard: 'Easy, you know, does it, son.'

The novel is one of Nabokov's most important statements. It tells us what his art has come to be about, and by analogy tells much more, surrounding the sorry story discretely and obliquely with an infinitely richer sense of something, some reality beyond the prison. Like the slightly preposterous Mr R.'s *Tralatitions*, or metaphors, *Transparent Things* is itself a metaphor, as are all his novels, suggesting that they are models designed to comment on a subject that exceeds their scope – a subject Nabokov hints at more clearly here than he has ever done before. The suggestion is that art itself is a metaphor for something that exceeds it – the relationship between ourselves, as prisoners of our reality, and whatever may lie beyond. A lunatic Person once met pointed out that the fact of survival after death would not necessarily solve 'the riddle of being'. Nabokov does not claim to solve it either; but *Transparent Things*, one of his best books, at least provides a metaphor that might contribute towards its solution.

Look at the Harlequins offers a last comment on Nabokov the artist and pattern-maker, and his status. It is, among other things, a parodistic account of the life of a Nabokovian character who writes highly Nabokovian novels, and occasionally has the suspicion that he is not his own master, not as real, as self-sufficient as he would believe; he may be no more than the imperfect creation of a greater author still – Vladimir Nabokov. The patterns he creates in his works are not entirely of his own invention; they are the echoes of patterns greater and more perfect, those of his creator. This is clearly true of the works of Vadim Vadimovich, whose occasional intuitions and suspicions are demonstrably vindicated. The plots of his novels are manifestly inferior echoes of Nabokov's own works. But *Look at the Harlequins* has further implications. In the course of a lifetime's work

Vladimir Nabokov

Nabokov has declared an increasing awareness of a higher order of reality, one that transcends our own, and that we may occasionally glimpse, or aspire to glimpse, through our prison bars. *Look at the Harlequins* suggests that, as Nabokov's creation, Vadim Vadimovich stands to Nabokov, so perhaps Vladimir Vladimirovich Nabokov, for all his originality, art and genius, his creative freedom, may stand to someone else, a still mightier artist. So that his works, his *Gift*, his *Lolita*, his *Transparent Things*, are no more than the echo of a higher order of being that is itself the echo of an echo of an echo....

In *Speak, Memory* Nabokov extends the notion of the restricting prison of consciousness to include the restrictions of time itself, which cut him off from his past. Time must be denied or overcome in order to establish the truth, glimpsed by Godunov-Cherdyntsev – that nothing is ever lost, and that apparent loss is an illusion, the creation of a partial and blinkered consciousness. Time is a prison 'spherical and without exit'; its walls 'separate me and my bruised fists from the full world of timelessness'; and time is the very signature of consciousness. 'The beginnings of reflexive consciousness in the brain of our remotest ancestor must surely have coincided with the dawning of the sense of time.'

Artists have a privilege and a power that enables them, sometimes, to get a glimpse of something beyond our mortal limits. They get as near as any mortal can to transcending the limits, breaking out of the confines of a consciousness so formed that we can only see what it allows us to see. This is Nabokov's supreme achievement. Nabokov ends a lovely evocation of his dead mother with a passage that resumes the attitudes and aspirations of a lifetime:

> It is certainly not then – not in dreams, but when one is awake at moments of robust joy and achievement, on the highest terrace of consciousness, that mortality has a chance to peer beyond its own limits, from the mast, from the past and its castle tower. And although nothing much can be seen through the mist, there is somehow the blissfull feeling that one is looking in the right direction.

6 The Sublime and the Ridiculous: Nabokov's Black Farces

Martin Amis

There are several ways in which Nabokov's art still needs to be celebrated. His reputation is considerable, but it is the wrong kind of reputation; his admirers are many, but they are the wrong kind of admirers. Two years after his death Nabokov is still best known as the embodiment of his idiosyncrasies – the haughty schematist, the trilingual punster, the arty hybrid. Now, perhaps, is the time to point out, in naïve admiration, that Nabokov spins a jolly good yarn, with believable characters, a strong story-line, and vivid, humorous prose.

Many factors have contributed to this mis-emphasis, and American scholarship is one of them. Nabokov is by no means the ideal US academic writer – like, say, John Hawkes, whose teacher's-pet novels are dutifully stuffed with metaphor patterns, colour schemes and myth profiles which the lecturer then dutifully prises out again for the instruction of his students. But Nabokov's art is intricate, playful and many-layered – often seeming to tease and anticipate literary criticism – and grows increasingly so as it becomes more compacted in his later period. American scholarship connives too eagerly with Nabokov's gamesomeness, seizing on the prismatic element in his work. That element is there all right, along with everything else; but it is quite non-central.

What is central about Nabokov is that he does all the usual things better than anybody else. In the end he looks as much Russian as American, with his delight in doleful strangeness and his unwavering – though riskily stretched – moral concern. Above all, Nabokov's style, which has alienated and infatuated so many readers, emerges not as a fancy appendage but as the key to his perceptual mode, his tireless attempt to pay full justice to the weird essence of things. Nabokov also has a distinctive modernity in that all his books are to some extent 'about art'. In a way this is simply a tautology: anyone who writes like Nabokov does is automatically writing about writing. However, one can quickly reassure sceptical readers that the theme is carried by Nabokov with unique sympathy and lightness – and, besides, art is no longer quite the subject it once was. Nabokov was an innovator, but he will soon seem exemplary. It is time, at any rate, that he was rescued for the mainstream.

'The Black Farces': this is a fairly arbitrary grouping, intended as an area of emphasis rather than a pigeon-hole. The three basic texts are *King, Queen, Knave* (1928), *Laughter in the Dark* (1932), and *Despair* (1934) – leading, as everything in Nabokov leads, to *Lolita* (1959), that terminal black farce, that miracle of thwarted energy. The three early novels resemble one another obviously and inescapably – they are all about murder, obsession, adultery, and perverse love; and they are all set in Weimar Berlin – yet the canon might easily be added to. *The Eye* (1930), for instance, though rather crystalline and remote, has strong chronological and topographical claims for inclusion; and as late a novel as *Transparent Things* (1972) is in some respects an abstract, masque-like black farce, relating to the early books in the same way as *The Winter's Tale* relates to Shakespearean tragedy. The Berlin trio, however, is firmly realist in its bearings, and so clearly of a piece (a little cul-de-sac of the author's genius) that it had better be looked at in isolation.

Nabokov was twenty-nine when he published *King, Queen, Knave*, his second novel, two years after his first, *Mary* (1926), a sombre, rarefied study of émigré rootlessness and Russia-love. What turned the young Vladimir into the author of these three highly athletic and pitiless novels? The question is worth considering, if only to be dismissed with a shrug; and it is vital to remember that the black farces are as much the work of an American writer in his sixties as of a Russian one in his thirties (another curious link, this: of all his Russian novels, the black farces are the only books he took the trouble to translate himself, in 1968, 1961 and 1966 respectively, the others being entrusted to collaborators).* Nabokov was leading a vigorous existence in Berlin: he was teaching tennis, boxing,

* *King, Queen, Knave* is officially credited to Dmitri Nabokov 'in collaboration with the author'. Nabokov explains in the 1967 Foreword: 'By the end of 1966, my son had prepared a literal translation of the book in English, and this I placed on my lectern beside a copy of the Russian edition. I foresaw having to make a number of revisions affecting the actual text of a forty-year-old novel which I had not reread ever since its proofs had been corrected by an author twice younger than the reviser. Very soon I asserted [sic] that the original sagged considerably more than I had expected.' Nabokov spent three months on the revision; the result has a sustained verbal intensity quite absent from the other Dmitri/Vladimir collaborations. It is Nabokovian to the letter.

languages; he had recently married the serene and formidable Véra (the dedicatee of all his books); and he was advancing his reputation in the tightly knit, almost hermetic émigré intellectual community (despite his linguistic gifts, Nabokov coolly declined to learn German, in order to get his Russian novels safely 'out of the way'). *Speak, Memory*, of course, maintains complete silence on the vulgar topic of autobiographical prompting; but there is a passably ingenuous paragraph about the émigré's attitude to his foster-home:

> As I look back at those years of exile, I see myself . . . leading an odd but by no means unpleasant existence, in material indigence and intellectual luxury, among perfectly unimportant strangers, spectral Germans and Frenchmen in whose more or less illusory cities we, émigrés, happened to dwell. These aborigenes were to the mind's eye as flat and transparent as figures cut out of cellophane... but occasionally, quite often in fact, the spectral world through which we serenely paraded our sores and our arts would produce a kind of awful convulsion and show us who was the discarnate captive and who the true lord.

That last phrase hints at the socio-sexual power-struggles, and the voiding insecurities, with which the black farces make such enjoyable play; more evocative still, though, is the remark, 'as flat and transparent as figures cut out of cellophane'. It suggests something about the stark surfaces of the black farces, and incidentally points to another mild happenstance that unites them. Not only do they use cinematic methods and explore cinematic themes, they are also the only Nabokov novels that have been made into films: Skolimowsky's *King, Queen, Knave*, Richardson's *Laughter in the Dark*, Fassbinder's *Despair* – and, by extension, Kubrick's *Lolita*. It would be easy to elaborate here on the way the black farces accelerate, retard and disarrange time; and on the two-dimensional directness with which they deploy terror, wincing laughter, and mad clarity.

Thunderheads, bad eyesight, nausea, migraine, false dusks, unseasonal weather, states of waking and half-sleep, carrion, coincidence, inventions, mirrors: these are the subliminal watermarks of the black farces. Emptiness, deceit, cupidity, deracination, dreams and death provide their energies. The character-scheme is unvarying (though the point of focus is not): there is a king (the breezy cuckold), there is a queen (the king's erring consort), and there is a knave (the subversive interloper). The literary mode is a perfectly recognizable one; and it is surprising that Nabokov's work has so seldom been considered in its light – that of the sublime, the sublime directed at our fallen world of squalor, absurdity and talentlessness. Sublimity replaces the ideas of motivation and plot with those of obsession and destiny. It suspends moral judgements in favour of remorselessness, a helter-skelter intensity. It does not proceed to a conclusion so much as accumulate possibilities of pain and danger. The sublime is a perverse mode, by definition; but there is art in its madness. Nabokov was attracted to the sublime because his style led him there: it inflamed his imagination, and dared his prose to stay abreast.

A helpful way into these books might be to highlight their implausibilities. *King, Queen, Knave* offers us, at the outset, a comfortable, childless, passionless married couple of the Berlin *nouveau riche*. It consists of Dreyer, a droll, cultured speculator and emporium-owner (who made his money from witty gambles during 'the inflation'), and Martha, his frigid, bad-tempered, 'madonna-like' wife. Nabokov captures the rhythm and texture of their life together early on, in one of his most pellucid passages. The wealthy couple lazily prepare for an evening out:

> Somewhere a door closed softly, and the stairs creaked (they were not supposed to creak!), and her husband's cheerful off-key whistle receded out of earshot. 'He is a poor dancer,' thought Martha. 'He may be good at tennis but he will always be a poor dancer. He does not like dancing. He does not understand how fashionable it is nowadays. Fashionable and indispensible.'... She thrust her head through the soft, gathered circumference of the dress. Its green shadow flew downward past her eyes. She emerged erect, smoothed her hips, and suddenly felt that her soul was temporarily circumscribed and contained by the emerald texture of that cool frock.
>
> Below, on the square terrace, with its cement floor and the purple and pink asters on its wide balustrade, Dreyer sat in a canvas chair by a garden table, and with his open book resting on his lap gazed into the garden. Beyond the fence, the black car, the expensive Icarus, was already waiting inexorably.... A cold late-afternoon lucency penetrated the autumn air; the sharp blue shadows of the young trees stretched along the sunny lawn, all in the same direction as if anxious to see which would be first to reach the garden's white lateral wall.... The shadow seemed to have moved just a bit farther but the sun still bore down triumphantly on the right from behind the corner of the count's villa, which stood on higher ground with taller trees. Tom [the dog] walked indolently along the flowerbed. From a sense of duty and without the least hope of success, he started after a low-flitting sparrow, and then lay down by the wheelbarrow with his nose in his paws. The very word terrace – how spacious, how cool! The pretty ray of a spiderweb

stretched obliquely from the corner flower of the balustrade to the table standing beside it. The cloudlets in one part of the pale clean sky had funny curls, and were all alike as on a maritime horizon, all hanging together in a delicate flock. At last ... the gardener moved off with his wheelbarrow, turning with geometrical precision at the intersections of gravel paths, and Tom, rising lazily, proceeded to walk after him like a clockwork toy, turning when the gardener turned. *Die toten Sùeelen* by a Russian author, which had long been slipping down Dreyer's knee, slid on to the flags of the floor, and he felt too lazy to pick it up.

Into this frozen, determinist Eden, with its obligations and sacraments (dancing is 'indispensible'; Martha's soul is 'circumscribed'; the car is 'inexorable'; the sun is 'triumphant' – even the clockwork dog acts from 'a sense of duty'; and the book sliding down Dreyer's lap is called *Dead Souls*), comes Franz, Dreyer's nephew, a gawky, stupid, squeamish, smelly, humourless, myopic provincial adolescent, full of the usual nervous greeds and lusts, but denatured by reflexive dreads about sin, guilt and poverty. Within fifty pages, fashionable Martha and charmless Franz are very energetic lovers; and within fifty more they are planning Dreyer's murder.

Why does Martha 'take' Franz as a lover – sordid Franz, who washes his feet twice a week and 'hardly ever skipped his Saturday bath'? ('The poor boy stank like a goat. And those long drawers on a day like this!' muses Dreyer carelessly, as, towards the end of the book, he helps Franz change into tennis gear.) And why do they proceed towards murder? Actually, the pair of them behave, in a sense, with almost impeccable conventionality throughout. Martha takes a lover because lovers are fashionable, fashionable and indispensible; yokel Franz responds to Martha as part of the promise of fabulous Berlin (described in coruscatingly feminine terms by Nabokov, always through Franz's defective irises). Murder – which, again, Martha envisages purely in terms of genre convention (poison, garotte, a magic gun: blissful release) – is the obvious fulfilment of their carnal, meaningless, conventionally sublime passion. The first thing Martha notices and likes about Franz is that he resembles 'warm, healthy young wax that one can manipulate and mould till its shape suits your pleasure'. So Martha indulges her 'mad passion', and Franz follows grimly in her wake: they go mad together, in fact, like the automatons they have become.

Dreyer is interested in automatons, too, but in a playful, dilettante-ish context. In common with the other kings in the black farces, Dreyer is an artist *manqué*, embodying two traits much execrated by Nabokov: presumptuous talentlessness and creative blasphemy. Dreyer's pet venture during the action of the novel involves the funding of innovatory mannequins, made out of a pliable, responsive new substance called 'voskin' (*vosk* is Russian for 'wax' – the same 'healthy young wax' that Franz is made out of). The hoped-for virtue of these lucrative toys is that they will be able to ape nature at the prompting of their manipulator (in this case the mad inventor whom Dreyer patronizes). As Martha's murder plans develop, Franz, too, subsides into a condition in which 'human speech, unless representing a command, was meaningless'. Franz, the knave, the would-be opportunist, is drawn on to the rack of the black farce, with its absurd, and absurdly intense, sufferings – as Martha is later on, fortuitously but fatally, while Dreyer, the cuckold, the dupe, is allowed to survive the novel in ignorance.

A further nightmare is added to Franz's tortures and to the book's argument about enervation and will. Embroiled Franz crawls through his days, existing 'only because existing was the proper thing to do.... His day ran its course automatically but his nights were formless and full of terror.' Franz sleeps alone in his boarding-house, under the crazed auspices of Enricht, the landlord. The steady emergence of Enricht's madness monitors Franz's own descent to the underside. (On the night that Franz funks his first chance with Martha he returns to his room and hears a chuckle from behind Enricht's door: he looks in to find his landlord squatting over a mirror, 'peering back through the archway of his bare thighs at the reflection of his bleak buttocks'.) It transpires that Enricht is under the impression that he, Enricht, is the famed illusionist and conjuror Menetek-El-Pharsin, and has, among other skills, the ability of transforming himself into all kinds of creatures – 'a horse, a hog, a six-year-old girl in a sailor cap'. On the night before Franz leaves his lodgings – to go to the seaside with the Dreyers, where the murder will be committed – Enricht complacently reflects on the potency of his own black arts.

> For he knew perfectly well ... that the whole world was but a trick of his, and that all those people – Franz, Franz's lady friend, the noisy gentleman with the noisy dog [Dreyer], and even his own, Pharsin's wife, a quiet little old lady in a lace cap, and he himself ... owed their existence to the power of his imagination and suggestion and the dexterity of his hands.... He knew perfectly well that there was no Franz behind the door, that he had created Franz with a few deft dabs of his facile fancy.

Enricht is an early embodiment of a theme that becomes more pressing as the black farces develop, and is also an example of Nabokov's peculiarly courteous modernity. For all his freakishness, Enricht is a realistic creation, who would not disconcert a contentedly realistic reader. Yet we are at liberty to notice that Enricht's ghastly thoughts suddenly make good sense if transferred to another personage in the wings of the novel: Nabokov himself. Is Franz behind the door? Only if Nabokov puts him there.

The next morning Franz awakes and prepares to leave for his grim holiday. The little scene is very Nabokovian: it represents the psychological, thematic and artistic pinnacle of the book – and it describes a young man getting dressed. (It is necessary to quote again at length, if only to acquaint the reader with the lavish, inordinate delights that are a matter of page-by-page routine throughout the black farces as nowhere else in Nabokov's work.) Typically, too, the passage combines horror with grotesque humour, showing Nabokov's quirky love for the duplicity of everyday objects when perceived through mutinous senses. It has the quality of all Nabokov's landscapes: everything in it is alive.

The waking hour struck. With a scream, shielding his head with his arms, Franz leapt off the bed and rushed to the door; there he stopped, trembling.... He had slept in his day shirt and had sweated profusely. His clean linen was already packed and anyway it was not worth the trouble of changing. The washstand was bare except for the thin relic of what had been a beige cake of violet-scented soap. He spent a long time scraping up with his fingernail a hair that was stuck to the soap; the hair would assume a different curve but refuse to come off. Dry soap collected under his fingernails. He started to wash his face. That single hair now stuck to his cheek, then to his neck, then tickled his lip.... There was no point in shaving. His hairbrush was packed but he had a pocket comb. His scalp felt scaly and itched. He buttoned up his wrinkled shirt. Never mind. Nothing mattered. Trying to ignore loathsome contacts, he attached his soft collar, which immediately grasped him round the neck like a cold compress. A broken fingernail caught in the silk of his tie. His second-best trousers, which had lain where they had been shed, at the foot of the bed, had gathered some nameless fluff. The clothes brush was packed. The ultimate disaster occurred while he was putting on his shoes: a shoelace broke. He had to suck the tip and ease it into its hole with the result that the two short ends were diabolically difficult to make into a knot. Not only animals, but so-called inanimate objects, feared and hated Franz.

At last he was ready.... He donned his raincoat and hat, responded with a shudder to his reflection in the mirror, picked up the suitcases, and, bumping against the doorjamb as if he were a clumsy passenger in a speeding train, went out into the corridor....

He stopped in the passage, stunned by an unpleasant thought: good manners bade him take leave of old Enricht. He put down the suitcases and knocked hurriedly at the landlord's bedroom door. No answer. He pushed the door and stepped in. The old woman whose face he had never seen sat with her back to him in her usual place. 'I'm leaving; I want to say good-by,' he said, advancing toward the armchair. There was no old woman at all – only a gray wig stuck on a stick and a knitted shawl. He knocked the whole dusty contraption to the floor. Old Enricht came out from behind a screen. He was stark naked and had a paper fan in his hand. 'You no longer exist, Franz Bubendorf,' he said dryly, indicating the door with his fan.

Franz bowed and went out without a word. On the stairs he felt dizzy. Setting down his load on a step, he stood clutching the banister. Then he bent over it as over a ship's side and was noisily and hideously sick. Weeping, he collected his valises, re-clicked the reluctant lock. As he proceeded downstairs, he kept meeting various traces of his misadventure. At last the house opened, let him out, and closed again.

Laughter in the Dark, published four years after *King, Queen, Knave*, is commonly regarded as the nastiest of Nabokov's novels, which is convenient in a way, because the nastiness of art is one of its principal themes. Certainly the book is his most despotic performance: unlike the other farces, it reads with a sense of escalation and inevitability, and with a calm relish of the spectacular humiliations that its hero is obliged to undergo. On page 1, Nabokov encapsulates the whole story with a twinkly flourish, happily drawing attention to the banality of the tale. 'Once upon a time' a rich and happy man left his wife for a young mistress: '... he loved; was not loved; and his life ended in disaster. This is the whole of the story and we might have left it at that had there not been profit and pleasure in the telling; and although there is plenty of space on a gravestone to contain, bound in moss, the abridged version of a man's life, detail is always welcome.' Nabokov's 'pleasure in the telling' is never more palpable. As narrator, he is a malevolent force in the book, inciting the energies of the evil characters and quelling the frail consciences of the weak.

Albinus, our king, a wealthy connoisseur, abandons his devoted and rather helpless wife for Margot, the usurping queen, an incarnation of vulgar meanness who, however, embodies the beauty for which Albinus yearns and is also (though Nabokov characteristically does not quite go into this) formidably talented in the sexual arts. Why does he do it? He just does it – as many men do, to find themselves living a cliché. Albinus's crime, in everyday terms, is lust combined with helpless, lust-induced sentimentality; but his crime in the grammar of the novel is again the crime of the artist *manqué*. Albinus searches for beauty in the human world (glimpsed girls leave in him 'that hopeless sense of loss which makes beauty what it is . . . a thing quite impossible to capture') and so misunderstands the place of art in that human world: 'Albinus's speciality had been his passion for art; his most brilliant discovery had been Margot.' (Conversely, the scheme that initiates his downfall involves 'animating' the Old Masters in cartoon form, an attempted travesty that parallels Dreyer's hubris.) Now Axel Rex, the knave, for all his exhaustive loathsomeness (as a child he set fire to live mice, and never looked back), *is* a genuine artist: '. . . at the same time this dangerous man was, with pencil in hand, a very fine artist indeed'. And cruelty, for Rex, is simply a refinement of the art of caricature. Delightedly expanding on Rex's delinquencies, his 'superhumour' wherein art subverts and derides life, Nabokov slyly invites us to identify Rex's role with his own:

[Rex] watched with interest the sufferings of Albinus . . . who thought, poor man, that he had touched the very depths of human distress; whereas Rex reflected – with a sense of pleasant anticipation – that, far from being the limit, it was merely the first item in the programme of a roaring comedy at which he, Rex, had been reserved a place in the stage manager's private box. The stage manager of this performance was neither God nor the devil. The former was far too grey, and venerable, and old-fashioned; and the latter, surfeited with other people's sins, was a bore to himself and to others as dull as rain . . . in fact, rain at dawn in the prison court, where some poor imbecile, yawning nervously, is being quietly put to death for the murder of his grandmother. The stage manager whom Rex had in view was an elusive, double, triple, self-reflecting magic Proteus of a phantom, the shadow of many-coloured glass balls flying in a curve, the ghost of a juggler on a shimmering curtain. . . .

The Protean juggler recalls Enricht's fantasies of godlike dexterity and power; and the plangent image of the prison court clearly echoes Dreyer's musings in the murderers' gallery in *King, Queen, Knave*:

How much those simpletons were missing! Missing . . . the ability to look with curiosity on what was essentially boring. And then the final Bore: at dawn, breakfastless, pale, top-hatted city fathers driving to the execution. The weather is cold and foggy. . . . The condemned man is led into the prison yard. The executioner's assistants plead with him to behave decently, and not to struggle.

These are the reflections of morally wayward characters, certainly; but through them Nabokov points to his own method of moral focus, which is a sublime one. The prison court and the idiot express the banality (so far as the artist is concerned) of crime and punishment, of dumb transgression and matter-of-fact reprisal. But even in the present phase of literature, with its paraded fastidiousness about all exterior values, the novelist retains the instinct to correct the erring puppets he creates. How will he do this? Not by trite punishment or improbable conversion, not by candid censure, not by any process of penitence and redemption; and not, finally, by any displacement of the cautionary tale. Nabokov does it by rendering the imaginative possibilities as intensely, as open-endedly and as perilously as he can, and by letting his style prompt our choice.

G. M. Hyde, in his *Vladimir Nabokov: America's Russian Novelist* (one of the few books on Nabokov that is actually an asset), has a particularly strong chapter on *Laughter in the Dark*, where he examines the novel's inverted, or 'negatived', colour scheme (white is black and black is white – note the Russian title, *Kamera Obskura*) and its play on the myth of the Fall (Margot twice compared to a snake; Rex, when discovered torturing the blinded Albinus, covering himself like Adam). Hyde's most useful contribution, though, is his delineation of the book's Tolstoyan thread. Tolstoy is summoned throughout *Laughter in the Dark*, not in the coltish way he is bounced off in *Ada*, but in order to elaborate on the artist's moral situation (the book is almost a running commentary on the late Tolstoy story, 'The Devil'). Towards the end of his life, of course, Tolstoy found himself disaffected by art's uselessness, seeing it as a system of palliative falsity and leisure-class gossip. But Nabokov knew that art, by celebrating suffering, also domesticates it. 'Art is a lie,' said Tolstoy. Nabokov would cheerfully agree – hence the innocuously rollicking agonies of *Laughter in the Dark*. Art is something else too, however, in Nabokov's thoroughly secular, contingent and relativized world. As Hermann Hermann says, halfway through *Despair*: 'To begin with, let us take the following motto (not especially for this chapter, but generally): Literature is love. Now we can continue.'

. . . . .

Reading through the Berlin farces consecutively, one duly notes their cross-currents and tics. There are the familiar coquettish jokes relating the novels (in addition to Nabokov's anagrammatic walk-ons): Hermann Hermann and Dreyer both drive the same 'expensive' Icarus, and in *Laughter in the Dark* Albinus is on easy social terms with his fictional predecessors. ('An invitation for lunch from the Dreyers. How nice.') And there are bolder reiterations of character and theme. The figure of the impenetrably smug cuckold, for instance: droll Dreyer never remotely suspects that he wears the horns, Albinus does so only after he has been annihilated by that fact, and Hermann goes one further – *he* never suspects either, although, as narrator, he is our only informant on the deception. Then, too, there is the uniformity of the women characters, all of whom – and appropriately so for the purposes of these fictions – are clichés of puerility, lust and greed (Margot is the smartest by some distance). The farces weave in and out of one another very insistently, yet without any sense of restatement or of unsavoury preoccupation.

The reason for this is partly technical. *King, Queen, Knave* is, in every respect, a third-person novel, entering the three protagonists' minds with impartial scrupulousness. *Laughter in the Dark* is a mixture of localized third-person (much of the action is seen through Albinus's eyes, though of course Albinus is too blinkered to be trusted with more than a moiety) and omniscient but personalized narrator (Nabokov the chuckling puppeteer). *Despair*, logically enough, is straight first-person, and takes us further into a mad mind than *Lolita* or even than *Pale Fire* – where we at least have Shade's poem as a constant, for all Kinbote's convolutions. Developing the theme of the artist *manqué* to an almost absurdist extreme, *Despair* itself is the narrator's attempted work of art, and the narrator, Hermann, has important disqualifications for creating art at all. Perhaps a personal note might help us to highlight the sort of radical dislocations that ensue. The first two times I read *Despair* I was astonished by the weakness of its ending: the last thirty pages were all wrong, the prose became digressive and off-centre, something slackened just as it should have tightened. Reading the early chapters for the third time, it occurred to me that the novel *had* to end weakly, as the final stamp of the narrator's sterility. I read on – and the ending no longer seemed weak: it seemed strong, triumphant, not just audacious and brilliant but gripping and totally satisfying. Would Nabokov have dared to approach the novel with this in view? I would not put it past him.

The action of *Despair* turns on a simple and splendid joke. Hermann, having reached a point of restless disgust with his own life, happens upon a sleeping tramp whom, he imagines, he astoundingly resembles. Hermann keeps in touch with the tramp – mawkish, whimsical Felix – while contemptuously reviewing the stage his life seems to have reached (in funny, knowing, disdainful prose, very like Humbert Humbert's, as Nabokov has acknowledged, though quite lacking in Humbert's mocking self-awareness: Hermann Hermann has no idea he is mad). Like Dreyer, he is 'a second-rate businessman with ideas'. He has a fat fool of a wife, Lydia, who for some reason gives a lot of her time to her cousin Ardalion, a 'talentless' painter. In fact, Lydia and Ardalion are clearly having an extremely vigorous affair, though Hermann is too self-absorbed and self-infatuated to notice. Here is an indication of the odd angle at which the world strikes him:

One November evening, especially, stands out in my memory: upon coming home from the office, I did not find my wife in – she had left me a note saying she had gone to the movies. Not knowing what to do with myself I paced the rooms and snapped my fingers; then sat down at my desk with the intention of writing a bit of fine prose, but all I managed to do was to beslobber my pen and draw a series of running noses; so I got up and went out, because I was in sore need of some sort – any sort of intercourse with the world, my own company being intolerable, since it excited me too much and to no purpose. I betook myself to Ardalion; a mountebank of a man, red-blooded and despicable. When at last he let me in . . . I caught myself wondering why I had come here at all.

'Lydia is here,' he said, revolving something in his mouth (chewing gum as it proved later). 'The woman is very ill. Make yourself comfortable.'

On Ardalion's bed, half dressed – that is, shoeless and wearing only a rumpled green slip – Lydia lay smoking.

'Oh, Hermann,' she said, 'how nice of you to think of coming. There's something wrong with my tum. Sit down here. It's better now, but I felt awful at the cinema.'

'In the middle of a jolly good film, too,' Ardalion complained. . . .

'Look here,' I said, turning to Ardalion, 'surely I am not mistaken; you have painted, haven't you, such a picture – a briar pipe and two roses?'. . . . [Hermann searches unsuccessfully for the painting.]

'Well,' Ardalion inquired, 'found it?'

Shook my head. Lydia had already slipped on her dress and shoes and was in the act of smoothing her hair before the mirror with Ardalion's hairbrush.

'Funny – must have eaten something,' she said. . . .

'Just wind,' remarked Ardalion. 'Wait a moment, you people. I'm coming with you. I'll be dressed in a jiffy. Turn away, Lyddy.'

He was in a patched, colour-smeared house-painter's smock, coming down almost to his heels. This he took off. There was nothing beneath save his silver cross and symmetrical tufts of hair. I do hate slovenliness and dirt. . . . Lydia looked out of the window and kept humming a little song which had long gone out of fashion (and how badly she pronounced the German words). . . .

He had supper with us, then played cards with Lydia and left after midnight. I offer all this as an example of an evening gaily and profitably spent. Yes, all was well, all was excellent, I felt another man, refreshed, renovated, released. . . . I cannot refrain from giving as well an instance of my literary exercises – a sort of subconscious training, I suppose, in view of my present tussle with this harassing tale. . . .

All the passions of the black farces – their obsessions, duplicities and drives – are subsumed in Hermann's relationship with himself. And Hermann is a Russian, with all the additional pains of exile. Hermann being Hermann, moreover, these pains include those of the Russian literary tradition: Hermann remains 'a superfluous man'.

Falteringly the plot proceeds. Hermann resolves to dress Felix, his 'double', in his own clothes, furnish him with his own passport, money, car – and murder him. Not only will he profit from the insurance money (in the conventional whodunit manner which the novel neatly parodies), he will also, he hopes, escape from his own obscurely tattered life. Hermann's dazzling plan, over which he gloats a good deal, has one rather serious flaw: Felix does not significantly resemble him. Holed up in a Swiss hotel, waiting for the police to come, Hermann starts to write his story, to write *Despair*, in explanation and atonement. This is how he begins, or tries to:

If I were not perfectly sure of my power to write and of my marvellous ability to express ideas with the utmost grace and vividness. . . . So, more or less, I had thought of beginning my tale. Further, I should have drawn the reader's attention to the fact that had I lacked that power, that ability, et cetera, not only should I have refrained from describing certain recent events, but there would have been nothing to describe, for, gentle reader, nothing at all would have happened. Silly, perhaps, but at least clear.

But it isn't clear, not yet. Sick Hermann equates his fatal perceptual flaw with the gift of literary talent. It is not a good start.

For *Despair* is flying about, *Despair* is disintegrating, as Hermann tries to write it. Hermann is not in control of his material: his material is in control of him. Everything to do with Hermann has equal value on the page (a fancy neologism, an irrelevant boast, a piece of paper falling from his desk, murder, his heartbeat) simply because it is to do with Hermann. His falsity, ruthlessness and solipsism are presented in terms of *literary* shortcomings. Whereas the genuine artist sheds his ego for his art – writing is after all a disinterested use of words – Hermann can find no exit from the squirrel-cage of the self. Eventually, of course, he commits the final travesty: he comes to see murder and art as equivalents, rather than opposites; exposed, he reads the newspaper reports of his crime as if they were hostile reviews, comforting himself with the thought that he is merely 'a poet misunderstood'. He experiments with various literary gambits to end his masterpiece; but they turn dead in his hands as trite and inexorable reality moves in – policemen, rain at dawn in the prison court, top-hatted city fathers, pale, breakfastless. No wonder the book ends with a whimper: Hermann's defeat is unqualified. But then so is Nabokov's triumph. With *Pale Fire*, *Despair* is his most technically self-challenging novel, and one of his most perfectly achieved.

In the 1965 Foreword to *Despair*, Nabokov speaks of 'the ecstatic love of a young writer for the old writer he will be some day'. In a secondary but parallel sense, the reader of the three Berlin farces can watch Nabokov getting ready to become the author of *Lolita*. The later book is not a 'development' of the black farces so much as a condensation of all their pain, laughter and intensity. (It is also a magical accident of subject and setting – Lolita and America, who both share that 'quality of wide-eyed, unsung, lyrical surrender'.) The decision to involve a lunatic failed artist and a twelve-year-old bobby-soxer in a novel about love – a love at once hopeless, blasphemous, infinite and unrequited – was an act of sublime impetuousness; but it was the sort of thing the black farces had led him to expect of himself. Everything Nabokov said about his art (in *Strong Opinions*, mostly) is as defeatingly dead-ended as the Preface to *Dorian Gray*; he chose his subjects for no other reason than that he thought he might write well about them. *Lolita* was the ultimate arena for his prose:

Thus, neither of us is alive when the reader opens this book. But while the blood still throbs through my writing hand, you are still as much part of blessed matter as I am, and I can still talk to you from here to Alaska. Be true to your Dick. Do not let other fellows touch you. Do not talk to strangers.... That husband of yours, I hope, will always treat you well, because otherwise my spectre shall come at him, like black smoke, like a demented giant, and pull him apart nerve by nerve. And do not pity C.Q. One had to choose between him and H. H., and one wanted H. H. to exist at least a couple of months longer, so as to have him make you live in the minds of later generations. I am thinking of aurochs and angels, the secret of durable pigments, prophetic sonnets, the refuge of art. And this is the only immortality you and I may share, my Lolita.

Writing about writing is a feature of twentieth-century literature that people are only beginning to resign themselves to. Actually, this apparent introversion is as much a matter of coincidence as of self-consciousness, and we ought to stop feeling puritanical about it. Until the present century there were things outside literature to which literature could seem to submit its ethical dealings. Now the Arnoldian prophecy has been fulfilled, and for the time being art is the only place for our spiritual intimacies. At its best, such writing can fill the place of the thing whose absence it mourns. At its worst, it is simply a new way of writing badly (only the prodigiously talented need apply). The main trouble, naturally, is that it is very hard to avoid being boring. Everyone thinks they are interesting about their work: it is an occupational hazard. Nabokov is never boring because he never loses his sense of play – but then, he had the living genius of the English language to play with.

7 Nabokov: Homo Ludens

Mark Lilly

Nabokov's work is a joke: that, at least, is a kind of crude shorthand for the idea that I want to explore in this essay. But in order to show properly how this can be so, we must take a brief look at the way critics have traditionally addressed themselves to questions about the nature of literature itself. Nabokov is such an unusual writer that it is difficult to avoid theoretical issues; but, put more positively, the reader may well find that a consideration of those issues is a positive stimulant to his interest in, and enjoyment of, the various novels.

If we look at the various theories of literature that have been advanced in the West from the ancient Greeks to the present day, a single basic assumption appears again and again. Indeed, no theory can be sound which does not take account of it. Aristotle, in his *Poetics*, explained this assumption by saying that art essentially has a double quality: it produces delight, but it also teaches the reader something. We can see this double function operating in the fourteenth-century Chaucerian bawdy tales, for example, which are splendidly amusing but also heavily moral. Ben Jonson expresses a typical Renaissance view when he says of plays that they 'ought always to carry a mixture of profit, with them, no less than delight'. Since then, the major theorists, people who have often contributed to, as well as described, our notion of what literature is – Dryden, Johnson, Coleridge, Arnold, Leavis – have all shown an awareness of the implications of this double function. We appear to have reached a point where it is so rooted in our idea of art that it is taken for granted and rarely mentioned explicitly. In order to find a useful notation for these two concepts, we can do no better than to adopt Horace's description of poetry as '*dulce et utile*' (sweet and useful).

Let me try to clarify the meaning of the two terms as I intend to use them. Under the heading *utile* we can gather such notions as art's social conscience, its documentary value, its pedagogic or didactic element; in this view, the individual novel or play is our teacher. On the other hand, *dulce* refers to our (assumed) enjoyment of the work – our thrill at a particular rhyme, our satisfaction in the turn of a plot and, in general, our aesthetic satisfaction.

Now, the proposition on which this essay is based is that Nabokov's work can profitably be viewed as an attempt to be rid of *utile* and to exalt *dulce* to spectacular heights. The ways in which this is achieved – so that the reader's enchantment and delight become the *raison d'être* of each novel – are richly diverse; but before we study actual examples, I need to say a little more about the theory.

In the late nineteenth and early twentieth century, certain writers and critics – one thinks of Oscar Wilde, but before him there was Théophile Gautier, and after him, Clive Bell – put forward the doctrine known as 'art for art's sake'. This held that novels, poems, and paintings should not set out to preach to the reader/viewer, or inform his social conscience. True art had nothing to do with messages: the powerful directness of Zola's social realism, the sophisticated intellectual morality of George Eliot, these were alike rejected. Clive Bell broadcast the doctrine with energy:

> Those who find the chief importance of art or of philosophy in its relation to conduct or its practical utility – those who cannot value things as ends in themselves or, at any rate, as direct means to emotions – will never get from anything the best that it can give. Whatever the world of aesthetic contemplation may be, it is not the world of human business and passion; in it the chatter and tumult of material existence is unheard, or heard only as the echo of some more ultimate harmony.

Readers of Nabokov's interviews (collected in *Strong Opinions*) will immediately recognize an extraordinary degree of congruence with Bell's position. There is, assuredly, an important difference of emphasis between Bell's categories of pure art and 'significant form' (implying, as they do, a sort of monastic exclusiveness) and Nabokov's commitment to delight the reader (and himself) at all costs. But the essential similarity is precisely that assault on instruction, or 'usefulness', which, as I have suggested, characterizes Nabokov's fiction. Nabokov, however, goes far beyond Bell's demand for the rejection of '*utile*'; his novels actually become games in which the readers are players, their task being to 'solve' the problems set by the games master-novelist. It is in this sense that we can properly refer to Nabokov as *homo ludens*: man the player.

The game-puzzles can usefully be divided into two broad

categories. First, there are the hundreds of individual puns, acrostics, anagrams, and other verbal devices that are local and specific. Proper names are typical of this category, and allow immediate satirical force: bric-à-Braques, Dusty (Dostoevsky), *All Quiet on the Don* ('a fusion of two cheap novels'). Certain writers get repeatedly lampooned, like T. S. Eliot in *Ada*: 'Kithar Sween, a banker who at sixty-five had become an *avant-garde* author; in the course of one miraculous year he had produced *The Waistline*, a satire in free verse on Anglo-American feeding habits, and *Cardinal Grishkin*, an overtly subtle yarn extolling the Roman faith.' Nabokov's non-satirical joke names are among his best: Dr V. V. Sector, Socrates Hemlocker, Mrs Arfour (that is, R4, a chess notation). These are immensely comic surface characteristics; but it is the actual structure of the works – this is our second category – that most effectively illustrates the notion of game. Alfred Appel has shown in *The Annotated Lolita* how important it is for the reader to assume the guise of a painstaking detective looking for clues; on one matter alone, the identity of Clare Quilty, Appel lists over forty 'references and hints' in the novel, some of which would only be picked up by a re-reader.

One of the best examples of a Nabokov novel requiring extensive reader detective work is *The Real Life of Sebastian Knight.* The narrator, whom we know only as V., is concerned to rectify what he considers to be the inaccurate biography of his novelist half-brother Sebastian Knight, written by a hack called Goodman. To this end, he travels from place to place following in his brother's footsteps, attempting to find the truth. What we are presented with, in fact, is Nabokov writing about V. writing about Sebastian (written about by Goodman) writing his own novels. And, of course, there are extensive passages from the work of these different writers: from Sebastian's novels and Goodman's biography. There are analogous situations in literature – in *Wuthering Heights*, Emily Bronte gives us Lockwood quoting Mrs Dean quoting Heathcliff, for example; but confusion is avoided by making the relation between the different levels quite clear. Nabokov deliberately confuses those relations, so that nothing can be asserted for sure. In reading the novel, we experience constant shifts of perspective, in trying to determine which writer – V., Sebastian, Goodman, even Nabokov – is reliable.

As we proceed, we notice similarities arising between V. and his half-brother: their style of writing is very similar; everything that V. does seems to duplicate Sebastian's actions – they both fall in love with Nina, for example; and, near the end, V. receives a telegram which refers to his half-brother as 'Se*v*astian'. Meanwhile, there are clues to connect Sebastian to Nabokov: Goodman's hack criticism of his subject's artistic talent is of the type that we know Nabokov himself particularly resented when used of his own work; they were both born in 1899; both went to Cambridge; both read and liked Housman and Rupert Brooke; both wrote under pseudonyms. Even Sebastian's surname, reminding us as it does of Nabokov's preoccupation with chess, is telling.

To add to this complexity, Goodman's biography certainly conflicts factually with V.'s memory of his half-brother – there is a discrepancy, for example, about whether Sebastian liked gambling or not; and V. himself shares traits with Nabokov, the suggestion of Vladimir in the V. being only the most obvious. We are, therefore, well prepared for the final unfolding: 'I am Sebastian, or Sebastian is I, or perhaps we both are someone whom neither of us knows.' What Nabokov achieves in this narrative conundrum is the debunking of the word 'real' (used ironically, of course, in the title) as a word with any feasible meaning. Instead, he creates out of the confusion between real and unreal his own delightfully enchanting world of creative deception. It is self-contained, solipsistic, requiring no external justification.

The kind of detective game represented by *The Real Life of Sebastian Knight* is evident in all Nabokov's novels, though not to the same degree. Works like *Despair* and *Transparent Things* crucially depend on the 'sleuth' quality of the reader; but novels like *Pnin* and *Mary* are not quite so demanding. The intricacy of V.'s narrative is based on that of multiple stand-points. This is also true of *Pale Fire*; the two central figures of John Shade and Charles Kinbote are in a complex relation to the poem and commentary of which they are, respectively, the authors. They also mirror each other in ways reminiscent of V. and Sebastian. In *Despair*, there is incongruity between what the (mad) narrator, Hermann, tells us, and what we infer to be the actual case. All three novels use the device known as the 'unreliable narrator'; this simply means that the reader does not take the purported facts and inferences of the narrative at their face value. As I have suggested, establishing the inconsistencies and contradictions by means of clues in the text can properly be thought of as a game for the reader. But unreliable narrative is not the only component of the novel-game. There is, for example, a series of devices –

doppelgängers, alter egos, mirrorings – that combines with the unreliable narrative to make the sorting out of identities additionally difficult.

Perhaps our sense of the Nabokovian game is at its sharpest when we are faced with the elaborate metaphorical and thematic harmony that makes of each work an organic whole. In the criss-crossing of references and allusions, in the imagery whose development is a subplot in itself, we sense the delight in puzzle-making that in turn spurs on the reader in his search for answers. The intricacy of Nabokov's maze, and the fun of finding oneself in it, are exemplified in *The Defence.*

The protagonist Luzhin is a rather pathetic figure, not unlike the absent-minded Pnin. He is hopelessly unsuccessful at human relations and thrives only in his professional life as a chess grand master. The novel is largely an account of how chess becomes an obsession in Luzhin's life and, finally, a threatening force. Nabokov's skill is in the elaboration of a scheme in which the whole of life is seen in terms of this game. Arithmetic is boring for the child Luzhin; and yet, in its black-white contrast, it prefigures that monochromatic mimic of the battlefield, the chessboard itself: 'The page with criss-cross blue lines grew blurry; the white numbers on the blackboard alternately contracted and broadened.' Increasingly, the physical world takes on the appearance of a chess force-field: 'The urns that stood on stone pedestals at the four corners of the terrace threatened one another across their diagonals.' Even courtship is seen as an opening gambit: 'Luzhin began with a series of quiet moves. . . .' He comes to grasp the dreadful truth – he is now himself a pawn: '. . . and when Luzhin left the balcony and stepped back into his room, there on the floor lay an enormous square of moonlight, and in that light – his own shadow.' It is not surprising that having at last resolved on suicide, he should tell his wife that he must 'drop out of the game'; the act of climbing through the bathroom window is obviously an image of escape from the 'squares' that have tormented him.

It is not merely the imagery of the novel that forms a harmonious whole. The organization of event sequences itself takes on a chess pattern; for example, the chronological to and fro of Chapters 4, 5, and 6 is as initially misleading as a deceptive chess manoeuvre during an opening gambit. I have always felt, however, that in this novel the most appealing fictional 'move' – because the most ingenious – occurs at the very end. That ending we shall now discuss.

Chess represents a battle between two opposing armies. The game ends when one of the kings is 'killed' – 'checkmate' comes from the Arabic '*shah mata*', 'the king is dead'. But no sooner is the game over than the king can be reinstated upright on the board for a further contest. Certain parallels exist between Luzhin and the chess king. Both are relatively passive compared to the pieces/characters around them; their tendency is to respond to situations, rather than initiate them. They will retreat before they will advance. Now, is not the spectacle of Luzhin being driven, as it were, into a corner (the bathroom) something like the concluding moves of a game of chess? Furthermore, just as the chess king is not really dead, neither is Luzhin. Readers who assume that Luzhin dies at the end of the novel are falling into a trap.

Let us consider that final scene. Locking himself in the bathroom, Luzhin smashes an upper pane of glass and climbs outside, hanging from one hand: 'Some kind of hasty preparations were under way there: the window reflections gathered together and levelled themselves out, the whole chasm was seen to divide into dark and pale squares, and at the instant when Luzhin unclenched his hand ... he saw exactly what kind of eternity was obligingly and inexorably spread out before him.'

The novel ends with Luzhin in mid-air. It is an important part of the way the final scene is written that the traditional practice by which readers imaginatively continue the story beyond the ending is debarred. I stressed at the beginning the importance of the idea of art for its own sake in Nabokov's novels. So much is this the case that, here, the novel must be said to end its life, as it were, on the final page, and readers are certainly to be discouraged from continuing the story in their own heads.

Luzhin must not be thought of as dead. Suspended over 'dark and pale squares', bringing together in his final act the dreamlike quality of life (made clear by the slow-moving, uninvolved tone of the prose passage quoted) and the reality of chess (in the image itself), Luzhin embodies a contradiction. Like the erotic power of a statue which, for all its sensuousness, is nevertheless cold marble; and like the dancing, chasing youths on some priceless vase who nevertheless do not, and can never, move, so Luzhin tumbles to a chessboard death that he will never reach.

I have used *The Defence* to illustrate what I termed earlier the metaphorical and thematic harmony in Nabokov's work. This feature, like the intricacies of narrative and identity, can readily be seen as game, in that it presupposes readers who are alert to clues, and eager to put them together in a meaningful whole. Because this is so, we can see how appropriate it is that in the novel's Foreword, Nabokov refers to his having 'planted' the chess effects.

At this point, I should like to widen the meaning of the term 'game', which hitherto has been used in its everyday sense. Because Nabokov does not wish his novels to moralize, he makes every effort to prevent them from being taken as such through an extravagant use of the unconventional. The novels then become so different from what we have learnt to expect in fiction, that we accept them on their own terms. Nabokov's devices succeed in making us view the novels as solipsistic and discrete entities. These unconventional devices – because they are part of the attempt to give us art as delight, because the reader's pleasure is so central in them – I now want to incorporate under the 'game' heading. It will be seen, anyway, that many of these devices are very much like games under the first definition.

Consider the opening paragraphs of *Laughter in the Dark*:

> Once upon a time there lived in Berlin, Germany, a man called Albinus. He was rich, respectable, happy; one day he abandoned his wife for the sake of a youthful mistress; he loved; was not loved; and his life ended in disaster.
>
> This is the whole of the story and we might have left it at that had there not been profit and pleasure in the telling; and although there is plenty of space on a gravestone to contain, bound in moss, the abridged version of a man's life, detail is always welcome.

This is a typically ironical opening designed to put off 'unsuitable' prospective readers, primarily interested in the onrush of the plot, or who seek emotional identification with the major characters. The famous opening paragraph of *Lolita* has a startling poeticality, which no doubt deters those in search of tabloid sensationalism. *Despair* begins with the narrator discussing various possible ways of beginning to write his account; and *Ada*, *Bend Sinister*, and *Look at the Harlequins* also have esoteric openings that might frighten away the casual browser. These openings give notice that the mode of telling, rather than the tale itself, must remain our proper focus; they are designed to purge us of conventional expectations. In the case of *Laughter in the Dark*, for example, Nabokov unsettles his reader by breaking the taboo that insists the outcome of the story should be kept secret.

Another relevant feature is the fantastic plot. We *must* treat as a joke, an indulgence, novels like *Ada* that feature flying carpets, those, like *The Real Life of Sebastian Knight*, where the characters' very identities are mysterious, or like *Invitation to a Beheading*, where reality is a stage-set which ultimately crumbles to nothing. The bizarre names of the protagonists – John Shade, Humbert Humbert, Albinus – contribute to this feeling.

Perhaps one of the most successful departures from convention is the deceptive ambiguity of character in the major protagonists. Some examples will make this clear. On the surface, Luzhin, in *The Defence*, appears as a figure especially designed to attract the warmth and sympathy of the reader; there he is, with his grubby handkerchief, his unwitting rudeness, his dazed unawareness of the world. He is endearing because of his helplessness, and because that helplessness makes him fall victim to the pain and anguish that disrupt his life. And yet Luzhin's inhuman coldness pulls us in the opposite direction, towards antipathy. He rejects his father's love; he is unaware of his kind aunt's sad involvement with the old man; he cannot grieve at the latter's death. A maniac intensity simply rules out all that is extrinsic to chess: 'Not a single picture could arrest Luzhin's hand as it leafed through the volumes – neither the celebrated Niagara Falls nor starving Indian children (pot bellied little skeletons) nor an attempted assassination of the King of Spain. The life of the world passed by with a hasty rustle, and suddenly stopped – the treasured diagram, problems, openings, entire games.'

I invite the reader to ask himself whether he can avoid a certain distaste for a boy whom starving children do not move. To describe Luzhin as callous is misleading, for, of course, he ignores his own interests as well as others'; for example, when his photograph first appears in the papers, 'Instead of the joy expected by his father, he expressed nothing.' Nevertheless, I view his character as a combination of endearing and unpleasant features, intended to prevent reader 'identification' (or its opposite). We are to view him merely as the centrepiece of Nabokov's game about a game.

A very similar technique is employed in *Bend Sinister* with Adam Krug. On the surface, Krug is a heroic scholar, resisting totalitarian pressure and refusing to sacrifice his principles. But this surface reading is subverted by the reader's growing awareness of what Krug stands for: the snobbish and the élitist. We find that Krug's resistance has its origin in bloody-mindedness, rather than in political humanism. At school, he is a bully; as an adult, he is grossly lascivious. The fate of personal friends, arrested to put pressure on him, seems to affect him little. And yet, indubitably, we applaud the fact of his resistance to the dictatorship of Paduk (the Toad).

As a final example, let us take the case of Humbert Humbert in *Lolita*. The discussion that took place twenty years ago about the 'morality' of the book took the predictable course. Supporters of the novel, knowing that arguments about literary merit cut little ice with public opinion, introduced the notion that, far from being an evil work, *Lolita* was actually an intensely moral parable. (This turning of the tables became a familiar feature of public and judicial consideration of *risqué* novels: witness *Lady Chatterley's Lover*, *Last Exit to Brooklyn*, *A Clockwork Orange*.) The word 'moral' could not be kept out: 'unflagging, moral' (Bernard Levin), 'highest moral purpose' (Terence Rattigan), even 'dreadfully moral' (Kenneth Allsop). But Lionel Trilling, predictably, had a more accurate version: 'For me one of the attractions of *Lolita* is its ambiguity of tone and its ambiguity of intention, its ability to arouse uneasiness, to throw the reader off balance, to require him to change his stance and shift his position and move one.'

This is precisely right; and I think that one way that we can account for this ambiguity and uneasiness is as follows: the facts of the novel are shocking, embarrassing, immoral; and yet the narrative has a casualness of tone, an improper lack of strong moral outrage. The murder of Quilty, and the attempts on Charlotte's life, are retailed with the calm deliberation we might associate with the description of a family picnic. What the philistine/prude really objected to was that Nabokov allows Humbert to have his say, to make a case. Even worse, both the deaths and the sexual scenes are hilariously funny; and it is precisely this type of grotesquerie that confuses the reader's moral assumptions. In *Lolita*, therefore, we find an incongruity between the immorality of deed, and the amoral way in which it is narrated, which creates the uneasiness that Trilling mentions. The ambiguity in the characters of Luzhin and Krug is in a similar way unsettling. This uneasiness certainly makes each reader conscious of a fresh approach to right and wrong. But its main purpose is not to replace one form of morality with a new one, but to direct us away from morality altogether, and towards the specially enchanted world where the logic and delight of games replaces everyday reality.

Nabokov relates an incident at the beginning of his autobiographical *Speak, Memory* that gives a very powerful indication of how far 'life' and its concerns are to be separated from the eclectic interpretations of art. As a rich child in St Petersburg, Nabokov was introduced by his father to General Kuropatkin, who tried to amuse the youngster by using matchsticks to represent, alternately, calm and rough seas. Fifteen years later, Nabokov's father, escaping to southern Russia, 'was accosted while crossing a bridge, by an old man who looked like a gray-bearded peasant in his sheepskin coat. He asked my father for a light. The next moment each recognized the other. I hope old Kuropatkin, in his rustic disguise, managed to evade Soviet imprisonment, but that is not the point. What pleases me is the evolution of the match theme.' In Nabokov's work the sadness of an old man, the transient joy of a reunion, are never the 'point'. This may be so partly out of a strong fear of appearing sentimental; but the main reason is a deliberate perversity that gives notice to the reader that the joys and sorrows of daily experience are put in second place, superseded by the more rarified aesthetic thrills of the game of art.

If we now turn our attention to the language itself, we find the same aspiration to pattern and form that is noticeable in the novels' structure. Consider, for example, this image from *Transparent Things*, intended to convey the idea of innocent curiosity: 'An African nun in an arctic convent touching with delight the fragile clock of her first dandelion.' All writers thrive on images; but there is an extravagance here, a boldness of comparison reminiscent of the metaphysical conceit, that is typically Nabokovian. The rhythm of the lines, too, is very marked, having a swinging regularity up to the word 'convent', and then changing tempo. The 'African/arctic' alliteration exploits the hard and soft 'a' to advantage; and the delayed 'd' and 'f' alliterations (in inverted order) are extremely subtle. But underlying all this is that familiar sense we have in Nabokov of the bizarre and the absurd. What does he mean by giving us such an image? As we relish the intricate pattern, we smile inwardly at the fact that it exists at all; and exploiting that contradiction in the reader's response is what Nabokov's linguistic virtuosity is all about.

Here is another extract, from *The Real Life of Sebastian Knight*, unusual in a rather different way:

> I know that the common pebble that you find in your fist after having thrust your arm shoulder deep into water, where a jewel seemed to gleam on pale sand, is really the coveted gem though it looks like a pebble as it dries in the sun of everyday. Therefore I felt that the nonsensical sentence which sang

in my head as I awoke was really the garbled translation of a striking disclosure....

That extraordinary rhythm is still there, particularly in the second sentence. But now we focus not on the striking quality of the terms ('African nun/arctic convent'), but on the idea itself. What we have, in fact, is a splendid twist to the pedestrian notion that appearances deceive. Nabokov takes it one step further by saying that the initial, imaginative perception has just as much right to assert its validity as any other. We must create our world inside our minds.

We have, then, a further illustration of our thesis that it is not 'reality' that matters, but what we make of it. Imagination, memory, artifice – these, typically, are the weapons in the Nabokov arsenal used to fend off the contingent and establish, in art, another world – a world of creative play, a zany kingdom of make-believe.

We might regard Nabokov's use of prose in these terms: he wishes to focus on the patterning of the words, so that they assume an abstract quality not unlike music. Unfortunately, words signify; they have levels of meaning that set us off on unruly tangential thoughts which threaten to disrupt the intricate pattern. In order to reduce this divergence from the abstract pattern of the work, Nabokov entertains us with the verbally unusual and spectacular. He makes language so self-conscious, so self-referential, that it becomes itself an object of scrutiny for the reader, whose attention thereby gravitates towards the mode of telling, and away from the tale. This, we remember, was part of the effect of the opening of *Laughter in the Dark* and similar devices.

Coming fresh to Nabokov, many readers find the loving presentation of minute detail to be among the most engaging features of the writing. Objects are noted not only with care; they are shown to us anew through comparisons at once vivid and delightfully bizarre: the moon 'glistened like a translucent nail clipping'; a character has an Adam's apple 'moving like the bulging shape of an arrased eavesdropper'; we hear of a clock showing 'the waxed moustache of ten minutes to two'.

The precision and freshness in these observations have not gone unmarked. In 1970, Simon Karlinsky wrote an article in which he compared Nabokov's work to Chekhov's; we are reminded that both men were scientists, professionally dedicated to minute examination; and this feature Karlinsky links to the striving of both writers to avoid overt political issues or moral formulas, their attempt to rise '*au-dessus de la mêlée*'. In other words, Nabokov's obsessive interest in detail (the microcosm) is one more diversion away from the supposedly more vital matters affecting the world at large (the macrocosm). Aloof from man's humdrum squabbles, the artist must make a record of the world; but it must be inspired by private magic, not by public prejudice. Part of Nabokov's private magic is the concept of game, which combines happily with the urge to observe and record. The narrator of *The Eye* seems to agree: 'And yet I am happy. Yes, happy. I swear, I swear I am happy. I have realized that the only happiness in this world is to observe, to spy, to watch, to scrutinize oneself and others, to be nothing but a big, slightly vitreous, somewhat bloodshot, unblinking eye. I swear that this is happiness.'

Let us draw our thoughts together, first by reminding ourselves of the argument thus far, and secondly by trying to arrive at some general conclusions. I have invited the reader to consider Nabokov's work as concerned with delight. The component of art that stirs men's consciences, or teaches them lessons, is suppressed. Nabokov achieves this delight by devising fictions that have the characteristics of games: they are fun on a surface level – jokes, anagrams, polyglot puns; and, on a deeper structural level, they require 'players' to work out 'solutions' – the complex plotting of, for example, *The Real Life of Sebastian Knight* and *Despair*. But Nabokov also 'plays' with his readers by sabotaging their conventional expectations. Thus, characters like Luzhin and Krug appear at times to be the sort of figures of whom we would normally approve; but at other times they seem repugnant. The obsession with patterning, the observation of detail, and the self-consciousness of language, are all ways of shifting attention from the humdrum contingencies of the outside world, and directing the reader inwards to the magical artifice that is the novel. With reality excluded, the good humour of the venture – without which no games can exist – is blissfully preserved.

It is now time to consider the two major objections to this way of looking at Nabokov's art. The first assumes the correctness of describing it as an elaborate game, and proceeds to condemn the whole enterprise as being trivial for that very reason. The second rejects the validity of the 'game' description, claiming that all good art will have a strong *utile* component, whether the writer intends it or not.

The critical view that 'play' is trivial frequently recurs. In looking over about thirty notices of the particularly innovative *Pale Fire* (1962), I found that, although reviewers were generally impressed by the skill displayed, they repeatedly protested that seriousness was lacking; that no novel could be 'great' unless it presented issues from the real world with less disguise. Cyril Connolly's reception was typical: 'an outstandingly original fantasy composed for the intellectually adult', but not 'great' in the sense in which we reserve that term for Flaubert, Proust, or Tolstoy. Greatness, Connolly argued, requires 'great events, great emotions or greatness in the author'. David Holloway wrote: 'But a great work of art? No. A good joke, unbelievably expanded? Yes.' Lawrence Lerner seemed almost resentful: 'Literature is not written in code, though thrillers are. Mr Nabokov is a comic writer of high talent, perhaps of genius; but he can go and play his cryptographic games on someone else, not on me.' Lerner's remarks, actually, are a good example of that extremity of claim which bedevils both the attackers and the supporters of Nabokov's fiction, and leads them into inconsistency. Surely Lerner would agree that many works, of which it might be assumed he approved, such as *The Waste Land*, are written 'in code'; and, what is more, in the same kind of erudite, allusive code as that used in *Pale Fire*.

What is the foundation for this low esteem accorded to fictive playfulness and, indeed, to comic modes in general? It may be that such an approach offends against the tyrannous orthodoxy of gloom; the prevailing *zeitgeist* is firmly rooted in despair; and anything like high spirits is almost a lapse in taste. We are not likely to be able to settle such an issue, that involves not only literature but our whole experience of culture in its widest sense. But it might be useful to draw attention to J. Huizinga's remarkable study of play, *Homo Ludens*. In particular, two initial premises hold an exciting relevance. First, Huizinga requires us to abandon a favourite tenet: that play, being inessential in terms of physical survival, constitutes (like language) one of the telling discriminations between man and other animals. 'Play', he writes, 'is older than culture, for culture, however inadequately defined, always presupposes human society, and animals have not waited for man to teach them their playing.'

The importance of this view is that it shows play not as an adjunct, but as one of the first and most basic conditions of the mind. The child plays before it thinks conceptually; *homo ludens* precedes *homo sapiens*. It would seem that man needs play to arrive at some accommodation with the world. Huizinga's second point is equally radical. His object is not 'to define the place of play among all the other manifestations of culture, but rather to ascertain how far culture itself bears the character of play'.

I have insufficient space here to explore the immense implications of this view of play. What we can say is that, if accepted, these views would tend to make us less likely to equate the 'game' with the trivial; they also indicate how far the play-element in Nabokov is – ironically – useful in helping the reader to come to terms with his environment. For, if Huizinga be right, and culture is itself to some degree a game, then literary works rooted in playfulness – through their complex structures and their aesthetic assumptions – provide the reader with a valid notation for his inner experience. This, of course, brings us to the second major objection to the play theory. If Nabokov's games, despite everything we have said so far, can actually be seen as useful, and if they might exercise a benign influence on a reader's mind, then the novels have a *utile* component after all. This objection is entirely valid. I still hold that the intention behind the works is what I have suggested from the beginning. But no novelist can legislate for his work, or prevent it from meaning different things at different times to different people. Many critics are, quite rightly, concerned to explore the moral and social content of the novels – for example, *Bend Sinister* as a political statement on totalitarianism, *Lolita* as a satire on American vulgarity; and Nabokov's personal intentions are neither relevant nor wholly ascertainable. Literature is common property; we interpret it as we will. This interpretation is informed far more by historical circumstance, individual judgement, and the state of literary taste, than by any authorial edict.

More fundamentally, it may be that the notion of separating the *dulce* and *utile* components is spurious. Aristotle suggests in the *Poetics* that our delight in art exists precisely because we are learning at the same time, 'gathering the meaning of things', in his phrase. It is useful in discussion to separate the two elements; but, in the end, we have to concede that it is neither desirable nor possible to produce literature in which *utile* is wholly lacking. Indeed, the presence of both might constitute a working definition of what literature is. I shall be content if the reader feels that Nabokov's work is a series of variations on the play theme, even if it is also many other things. To adopt a concise phrase from Northrop Frye, the games are not *the* whole *of* it, but *a* whole *in* it.

Vladimir Nabokov

Every aspect of Nabokov's play – the surface joke, the structural complexity, or the deliberately misleading technical innovation – in so far as it is delightful, seems particularly welcome in a time so insistent on heavy seriousness. Nabokov unfashionably offers his readers their own Forest of Arden in which to lose their anxieties for a while. Magus-like, he presides over an enchanted world whose individual details are sparklingly vivid, whose general mood is, typically, good-humoured, and whose labyrinths of guile provide a cherished holiday from care.

8 *Ada*, or the Perils of Paradise

Robert Alter

Ada occupies a problematically dominant place among Nabokov's novels. Twice as long as any other work of fiction he wrote, this ambitious, formally elaborate, fantastically inventive novel of his seventieth year was clearly intended as a culmination of the distinctive artistic enterprise to which he devoted half a century. In it he sought to incorporate and reach beyond the achievement of his two English masterpieces, *Lolita* and *Pale Fire* (both of which are abundantly alluded to in *Ada*). Or, to invoke a painterly analogy specifically brought to our attention several times in the novel, *Ada* is the third panel in a Boschean tryptich, a novelistic Garden of Earthly Delights that began with *Lolita* in 1954, in which there is a paradoxical fusion of lyricism and the grotesque, of free-wheeling invention and scrupulous attention to familiar reality, in which beauty flowers from perversion, a radiant dream of happiness from the shadow of loneliness and exile.

Lolita had been the most brilliant in the line of books that since the 1920s had studied the vertiginous intercrossings of imagination and reality, the artist and his world, through athletically allusive, involuted and parodistic forms. These same concerns were then given even more original and intricate formal expression in *Pale Fire*, while the new central emphasis in *Lolita* on the quest for a paradisiac past (Humbert Humbert's golden 'princedom by the sea') appeared in oblique refraction through Kinbote's longing for his lost kingdom. In *Ada*, as we shall see in detail, Nabokov moved boldly from a vision of paradise lost to one of paradise regained – or retained – for the first time in his fiction, though following the precedent of the autobiographic *Speak, Memory*; and he also produced the most capaciously encompassing of all his parodistic forms.

The result of this consciously culminating effort was, of course, greeted with cat-calls by the anti-Nabokovians as a supreme monstrosity of literary narcissism, and hailed with jubilation by the Nabokov loyalists as a climactic masterpiece. Re-reading *Ada* a decade after its publication, I find it a dazzling, but at times also exasperating, near-masterpiece that lacks the perfect selectivity and control of *Lolita* and *Pale Fire*. At the book's weaker moments, one feels that the novelist permits himself too much, inadvertently unravelling threads in his own rich tapestry through his eagerness to pursue every linguistic quibble, every gratuitous turn of a sexual or literary double meaning. In this last major work, Nabokov invented a hypothetical anti-world where everything culturally precious to him – the Russian, English and French languages, the vanished graces of his parents' aristocratic estate – could be harmoniously combined; and it may be that this embarrassment of riches encouraged a certain softness, made it more difficult for him to distinguish between imaginative necessity and private indulgence. But these recurrent capitulations to the temptations of mere byplay are the defect of a virtue; for the exuberance of the novel's more meaningful playfulness in fact brings it close to the crowning achievement Nabokov sought. Through many extraordinary passages, and in its larger design, *Ada* succeeds in illuminating in new depth and breadth the relation between art, reality, and the evanescent ever-never presence of time past; and it is that illumination that chiefly deserves our attention.

The dimension of parody, established with the first words of the text, has to be kept clearly in perspective; for nowhere else in Nabokov's writing is the parodistic mode made so pervasive and so deliberately obtrusive as here. Because parody is intrinsic to Nabokov's method, and because he more often parodies plot, situation and motif than style and narrative technique, a plot-summary of any of his novels is bound to be thoroughly misleading, but perhaps more so for *Ada* than for any other work. (To mislead the unsuspecting, of course, is precisely what he always intends: thus, the four concluding paragraphs of *Ada* are a pitchman's synopsis of the book, the prose of the novel followed by what the narrator, tongue in cheek, calls 'the poetry of its blurb'.) *Ada*, which, when it is going well, manages to be one of the sunniest works of fiction written in this century, sounds, to judge by the bare outlines of its plot, like a dark drama of fatal, incestuous passion. Van Veen, the retrospective nonagenarian narrator, has an ecstatic affair at the age of fourteen with twelve-year-old Ada, ostensibly his cousin, later discovered to be his sister. The two are irresistibly drawn to each other by their inner nature, but are separated by social taboo and the course of outward events. In the two decades from early adolescence to mature adulthood, the lovers enjoy four fleeting periods of illicit ardour together; but each time the subsequent separation is longer; and, while Van seeks the simulacrum of his Ada in a thousand whores and mistresses, both he and she are physically thickened and coarsened by the passing years, until at last they come together in late middle age, all passion not spent but certainly muted. In the background, moreover, of their partings and joinings, as the third, unequal angle of a thoroughly incestuous triangle, is the pathetic figure of Lucette, their mutual half-sister, who loves Van relentlessly body and soul, loves Ada, periodically, in a more strictly bodily sense, and finally destroys herself when she is rejected by Van.

All this may sound like rather lurid stuff, especially when one adds that there is a much higher degree of descriptive specification about sexual matters here than anywhere else in Nabokov's fiction. And it must be conceded that there are moments when the writer's sense of freedom in treating sexual materials leads to a certain gloating tone – most evidently, in the repeated evocation of an international network of élite whore-houses to which Van Veen becomes habituated.

In any case, the actual tenor of the novel as a whole is, of course, precisely the opposite of what this summary suggests. On a stylistic level, the seeming paradox is easy enough to explain: Nabokov's intricately wrought, elaborately figurative style, with its painterly effects and its perspectivist mirror-games, transmutes objects of description, even the most pungently physical objects, into magical *objets d'art*. When, for example, the narrator, in a spectacular set-piece, describes all three siblings in bed together (surely a parody of the *ménage à trois* grapplings that are stock scenes of pornographic literature), he invites us to view the action as though it were reflected in the ceiling mirror of a fancy brothel, and then proceeds to convert the rampant eroticism into a formal contrasting and blending of colours and movements. Physical details are not spared – 'the detail is all', Van Veen had affirmed earlier about the reality of all experience and memory; but, to cite a strategic instance, the exposed sexual fluff of redheaded Lucette and black-haired Ada becomes here a new-fledged firebird and an enchanting raven, varicoloured birds of paradise in a poet's Wonderland.

Nabokov has often been celebrated for his brilliance as a stylist; but it is important to recognize that this brilliance, perhaps most centrally in *Ada*, is not ornamental, as in some of his American imitators, but the necessary instrument of a serious ontological enterprise: to rescue reality from the bland nonentity of stereotypicality and from the terrifying rush of mortality by reshaping objects, relations, existential states, through the power of metaphor and wit, so that they become endowed with an arresting life of their own. An incidental samovar, observed in passing, 'expressed fragments of its surroundings in demented fantasies of a primitive genre'. Lucette drowning sees her existence dissolve in a receding series of selves and perceives that 'what death amounted to was only a more complete assortment of the infinite fractions of solitude'. Van Veen, driving through the Alps to his first rendezvous with Ada after a separation of fifteen years, sees from his flesh (to borrow an apposite idiom from Job) the palpable reality of time as his recent telephone conversation with Ada and his view of the landscape around him are transformed in the alembic of consciousness into a summarizing metaphor:

> That telephone voice, by resurrecting the past and linking it up with the present, with the darkening slate-blue mountains beyond the lake, with the spangles of the sun wake dancing through the poplar, formed the centerpiece in his deepest perception of tangible time, the glittering 'now' that was the only reality of Time's texture.

As a vivid commentary on what he aspires to achieve through style, Nabokov likens the youthful Van's astonishing agility in walking on his hands to the function of metaphor in Van's later work as a writer:

> It was the standing of a metaphor on its head not for the sake of the trick's difficulty, but in order to perceive an ascending waterfall or a sunrise in reverse: a triumph, in a sense, over the ardis of time.... Van on the stage was performing organically what his figures of speech were to perform later in life – acrobatic wonders that had never been expected from them and which frightened children.

We shall devote further attention later to those acrobatic wonders when we consider Nabokov's rendering of Ada and the paradisiac world of youth with which she is inextricably associated.

When one moves from effects of style to the larger narrative patterns of the novel, it is difficult to make full sense of the incestuous complications without attention to the ubiquitous use of literary allusion. In order to talk about the allusions, something first must be said about the setting. The principal action of *Ada* takes place, one recalls, in the late nineteenth and early twentieth centuries of a world alternately referred to as Antiterra and Daemonia, which has the same geography as our world but a teasingly different though parallel history. The area we call Russia having been conquered some centuries earlier by the Tartars, America has been settled by Russian as well as English and French colonists; and so Nabokov's own three native languages and literary traditions are able to flourish side by side, as complementary parts of a single national culture. From a terrestrial viewpoint – Terra the Fair, by the way, is a supposedly celestial place believed in mainly by the deranged on Antiterra – historical periods as well as cultural boundaries have been hybridized; the daemonian nineteenth century combines the quiet country houses of Chekhov and Jane Austen with telephones, airplanes, skyscrapers; a mock-Maupassant figure is contemporaneous with the author of a *Lolita*-like novel masquerading (anagrammatically) as J. L. Borges.

This device of a fictional anti-world gives Nabokov a free hand to combine and permute the materials of culture and history in piquant and suggestive ways, though perhaps, as I have already proposed, it also sometimes tempts him into self-indulgence; so that one begins to feel he is playing his games of anagrams, trilingual puns, coded hints and conflated allusions for their own sake, not because they have any imaginative necessity in a larger design. Vladimir Nabokov, that is, at times rather too closely resembles his anagrammatic double in the novel, Baron Klim Avidov, bequeathing ornate sets of super-Scrabble to the characters and, implicitly, to the readers. It must be admitted, though, that some of the incidental games, especially those involving literary figures, are amusing enough in themselves that one would hesitate to give them up. My own favourite is the treatment of T. S. Eliot, who appears as a truncated version of his own ape-necked Sweeney, 'solemn Kithar Sween, a banker who at sixty-five had become an *avant-garde* author; ... had produced *The Waistline*, a satire in free verse on Anglo-American feeding habits'; and who is seen, in most poetic justice for a versifier of anti-Semitic innuendoes, in the company of 'old Eliot', a Jewish real-estate man.

The most important advantage, in any case, that Nabokov gains through the freedom he allows himself to shuttle across temporal and cultural boundaries is that he is able to compress into the lifespace of his protagonist a parodistic review of the development of the novel. The story begins in the classic age of the novel; and, really, everything that happens occurs in purely novelistic time and novelistic space. Ardis Manor, where young Van Veen will meet Ada, is glimpsed for the first time, characteristically, in the following fashion: 'At the next turning, the romantic mansion appeared on the gentle eminence of old novels.' The narrative is frequently punctuated with such notations to remind us that everything is taking place against a background of familiar and perhaps jaded literary conventions, as the view shifts quickly, and not necessarily chronologically, from Romantic *récit* to Jane Austen, Turgenev, Dickens, Flaubert, Aksakov, Tolstoy, Dostoevsky, the pornographic novel, the Gothic novel, Joyce, Proust, and Nabokov beyond them. The 'plot', in fact, is from one point of view composed of a string of stock scenes from the traditional novel – the young man's return to the ancestral manor; the festive picnic; the formal dinner; a midnight conflagration on the old estate; the distraught hero's flight at dawn from hearth and home as the result of a misunderstanding; the duel; the hero's profligacy in the great metropolis, and so forth.

Though the technique of allusion is common to all Nabokov's novels, there is a special thematic justification for this recapitulation in parody of the history of a genre; for what Van Veen's story represents is a reversal of the major thematic movement of the novel as a genre. The novel characteristically has concerned itself with lost illusions – the phrase, of course, was used as a title by Balzac in a central work – from the quixotic knight who finally abandons his pursuit of a Golden Age, a broken man renouncing his chivalric vision and dying, to Flaubert's Emma, spitting out her daydreams of a blue Beyond in the last hideous retches of an arsenic suicide; to Anna Karenina – the first sentence of her story is quoted, in reverse, in the first sentence of *Ada* – ending her tortured love under the wheels of a locomotive. What 'happy endings' one finds in the classic novel are generally a matter of mere acquiescence to convention (Dickens) or sober accommodation of the protagonists to society (Jane Austen, George Eliot). *Ada*, in direct contrast, is an attempt to return to paradise, to establish, in fact, the luminous vision of youth and love's first fulfilment as the most intensely, perdurably *real* experience we know. It bears affinities to both Molly Bloom's great lyric recall of first flowering love at the end of *Ulysses* and to Proust's triumph over time through art in the last volume of his novel; but it is a more concerted frontal attack on Eden than either.

Two key allusions are especially helpful in understanding what Nabokov is up to with his incestuous lovers. One is simple, a mere negative parallel to serve as a foil; the other is complex, being a kind of imaginative model for the whole book and ramifying into other related allusions. Several passing references are made to Chateaubriand: Ada jokingly calls Van her 'René'; and the first half of the novel's title, *Ada or Ardor*, looks suspiciously like a parody of that most Romantic title, *René ou les Effets des Passions*. René, like Van, is a singular man with an artist's soul who enjoys the rare delights of bucolic ambles with his dear sister until the incestuous nature of her attachment to him forces them to separate. So much for the parallels; all the rest is pointed contrast.

René is a book suffused with Romantic *mal du siècle*; and René and Amélie, unlike the Veen siblings, are anything but 'children of Venus'; the paradisiac fulfilment of premoral desire is quite unthinkable for René and his sister, so that the very existence of such desire drives Amélie into a convent and ultimately leads to martyrs' deaths for both of them. In *Ada*, one can see from the sunlit River Ladore near the Ardis estate a view of Bryant's Castle (gallicized, *Château-Briand*), 'remote and romantically black on its oak-timbered hill'. The chief quality of Van Veen's world, by contrast, is brightness and intimate closeness, social and sexual, tactile and visual; and its oak trees, as we shall see, are part of a landscape very different from the dark romantic wood. René actively longs for death, even before the revelation of his sister's passion; he sees in it a hazy, alluring *ailleurs*, as though the concrete objects of this world could not conceivably satisfy the needs of his own swoon of infinite desire. Nabokov's hero and heroine, on the other hand, delight in the concrete particulars of this world – Ada is a naturalist, Van an artist – observe and recall them with tender meticulous care; and they both passionately love existence in this world, each being the other's ultimate point of anchorage in it, Van's male V or arrowhead (*ardis* in Greek) perfectly fitting into its inverted and crossed female mirror-image, the A of his sister-soul (ideogrammatists take note; Freudians beware).

The mirror play of Van's and Ada's initials – underscored at one point when Nabokov finds dramatic occasion to print the A upside-down – suggests that the two are perfect lovers because ultimately they are complementary halves of one self. Indeed, Van's book is really 'written' by the two of them, one imagination called 'Vaniada' expressing itself in two antiphonal voices. The birthmark on the back of Van's right hand reappears in exactly the corresponding spot on Ada's left hand, for both physically and psychically the lovers are really the two halves of that androgynous pristine human zestfully described by Aristophanes in Plato's *Symposium* and at one point explicitly alluded to by Nabokov. According to rabbinic legend, Adam in the Garden before the creation of Eve was androgynous; and it is clear that Nabokov, like the rabbis, has conjoined the Greek and the Hebrew myths, creating in his deliciously intertwined sister and brother an image of prelapsarian, unfragmented man.

A major clue to Nabokov's intention in this respect is the repeated allusion, especially in the Ardis section of the novel, to one of the most splendidly realized experiences of paradise in English poetry, Marvell's 'The Garden'. Adolescent Ada tries to translate the poem into French – in her version, an oak tree stands prominently at the beginning of the second line; after the lovers' first separation, the poem, most appropriately, serves as a code-key for the letters in cipher that they exchange. (The other code-key is Rimbaud's *Mémoire*, another ripely sensual poem of bucolic repose, rich in colour imagery, presided over by 'the gambol of angels'.) The second stanza of Marvell's poem, not quoted in the novel, begins as follows: 'Fair quiet, have I found thee here,/And Innocence thy Sister dear!/Mistaken long, I sought you then/In busie Companies of Men.' The lines are, of course, applicable point for point to the novel, a kind of adumbration of its plot, though both 'sister' and 'innocence' are given rather different meanings. Marvell's poem is a vision of bliss beyond the raging of physical passion. The solitary garden-dweller, however, does revel in the pleasures of the senses, luscious fruit dropping from the trees to delight his palate, while his mind withdraws into the happiness of self-contemplation where it – like the author of *Ada*? – 'creates, transcending these,/Far other Worlds, and other Seas'.

In *Ada*'s ardisiac setting, luscious fruit also comes falling from the branches, when the tree-climbing young Ada slips and ends up straddling an astonished Van from the front, thus offering him an unexpectedly intimate first kiss. In a moment Ada will claim that this is the Tree of Knowledge, brought to the Ardis estate from Eden National Park; but her slip from its branches clearly enacts a Happy Fall; for in this garden, as in Marvell's, no fatal sin is really possible. Marvell's poem also gives us a comic image of a Fall with no evil consequences: 'Stumbling on Melons, as I pass,/Insnar'd with Flow'rs, I fall on Grass.' The interlaced limbs of ardently tumbling Van and Ada are similarly assimilated to the premoral world of vegetation, likened to tendril climbers; and Van, rushing away from a last embrace of Ada at the moment of their first separation, is actually described as 'stumbling on melons', an allusion which would seem to promise that he will eventually return to his Ada-Ardis-Eden.

It is the concluding stanza, however, of Marvell's 'The Garden' that offers the most suggestive model for what Nabokov seeks to achieve in *Ada*. After the garden-dweller's soul, whetting and combing its silver wings among the branches, has experienced ecstasy, the poet glances backward at the first Adam's paradise, and then returns us to the 'real' world of time; but it is time now transfigured by art, nature ordered by 'the skilful Gardener' in a floral sundial to measure time. The industrious bee, then, no less than man, 'computes its time' (in seventeenth-century pronunciation, a pun on 'thyme' and thus a truly Nabokovian word-play) with herbs and flowers; time the eroder has been alchemized in this artful re-creation of paradise into a golden translucence, delighting palate and eye. Nabokov means to create just such an inter-involvement of art and pleasure transcending time, or rather capturing its elusive living 'texture', as Van Veen calls it; and this, finally, is the dramatic function of the novel's unflagging emphasis on erotic experience.

The point is made clearer in the novel by yet another allusion. Marvell's 'The Garden' modulates into several other poems in the course of the narrative; but the most significant is Baudelaire's 'Invitation au Voyage', which is burlesqued in the novel with an oak tree inserted in the second and third line, to establish the cross-link with Marvell. Baudelaire's poem is also a ravishing dream of a perfect world, a world saturated with both generally sensual and specifically erotic delight, but realized, as such bliss can only be realized, through the beautiful ordering of art. Against the background of the novel, the famous opening lines of the poem become an evocation of Ardis, Van addressing Ada: '*Mon enfant, ma soeur,/Songe à la douceur/D'aller là-bas vivre ensemble!/Aimer à loisir/Aimer et mourir/Au pays qui te ressemble!*' It is noteworthy that fragments of these lines are bandied about by Ada at the point in the narrative when their first sexual intimacy is recollected; significantly, this is the one moment in the novel when Ada actually says to Van that they are not two different people.

Baudelaire's poem, then, suggests what is also clear in the novel in other ways, that *Ada* is formed on the paradox of rendering the perfect state of nature through a perfect state of art, self-conscious, allusive and exquisitely ordered. In this respect, Nabokov also follows the model of Milton (who is burlesqued in tetrameters at one point) in the fourth book of *Paradise Lost*, where prelapsarian Eden is described through the most finely ostentatious artifice – a natural garden full of sapphire founts, sands of gold, burnished fruit, crystal-mirror brooks, in which the preceding literary tradition of envisioned paradises is incorporated through the cunning strategy of negation ('Not that fair field/Of Enna . . .', and so forth). It may be that *Ada* pays a price as a novel for being an extended poetic vision of Eden: Van and Ada sometimes seem to be more voices and images in a lyric poem than novelistic characters; the excess of formal perfection they must sustain makes them less interesting individually, less humanly engaging, than many of Nabokov's previous protagonists. In compensation, the expression in *Ada* of a lover's consummated delight in life and beauty is an achievement that has few equals in the history of the novel. Here is one brief but representative and thematically central instance, in which the lovers' present is juxtaposed with their ardisiac past:

> Her plump, stickily glistening lips smiled.
>
> (When I kiss you *here*, he said to her years later, I always remember that blue morning on the balcony when you were eating a *tartine au miel*; so much better in French.)
>
> The classical beauty of clover honey, smooth, pale, translucent, freely flowing from the spoon and soaking my love's bread and butter in liquid brass. The crumb steeped in nectar.

The honeyed bread-slice here is very much a Nabokovian equivalent of Proust's *petite madeleine* and, especially, of that more erotic tidbit, the ambrosial seedcake Molly Bloom puts from her mouth into her young lover Leopold's. Through its sweetness past and present fuse; or, to speak more precisely, they fuse through its sweetness minutely observed and recollected, then distilled into the lucid order of a poem that moves in alliterative music through a poised choreography of dactyls and trochees to the culminating metaphorical paradox of the honey as liquid brass and the final substitution of nectar for the honey, now become 'literally' food for the gods.

It is really for the experience of such moments – and there are many of them in the course of the novel – that *Ada* exists. To state this in generic terms, *Ada* is, in a rather precise sense of the word, Nabokov's most lyric novel. Characterization, certainly when compared with his own earlier fiction, tends to be abstract or schematic; and the operation of plot, always a source of fascination for Nabokov the ingenious craftsman, is somewhat problematic here, especially in the long telescoped period after Van's and Ada's youth. This is a novel about time, Van Veen repeatedly reminds us, which means that it is a novel about memory, a faculty that in Nabokov's view can serve us vitally only if we exercise the finest, fullest attentiveness to the life of each moment, and, ideally, the control of language required to focus the moment recalled. Nearly half-way through the novel, one character is described trying 'to *realize* (in the rare full sense of the word), . . . to *possess* the reality of a fact by forcing it into the sensuous center'; and a page later, the narrator, with continuing italic emphasis, goes on to say that such realization can be effected only through 'that *third sight* (individual, magically detailed imagination) which many otherwise ordinary and conformant people may also possess, but without which memory (even that of a profound "thinker" or technician of genius) is, let us face it, a stereotype or a tear-sheet'. *Ada* is a series of verbal experiments in making one *realize* in the rare full sense of the word. If a reader fails to see that, there is scarcely any point in reading the book at all; once attuned to this central purpose, he may find ample compensation for the incidental flaws.

In order to understand more concretely how this process of realization works in the novel, let us consider two further images of young Ada recalled (by her lover, of course, almost eight decades after the fact) to set alongside the moment of the *tartine au miel* we have already observed. Van remembers watching Ada during an evening game of 'Flavita' (Baron Klim Avidov's super-Scrabble) in the halcyon year of 1884:

> The bloom streaking Ada's arm, the pale blue of the veins in its hollow, the charred-wood odor of her hair shining brownly next to the lampshade's parchment (a translucent lakescape with Japanese dragons), scored infinitely more points than those tensed fingers bunched on the pencil stub could ever add up in the past, present or future.

This is beautiful; and it is also wittily complicated in a peculiarly satisfying way. The verbal portraitist is attentive to the fine modulations of colour, texture, and odour in his subject, with the oddly adverbial 'shining brownly' intimating the suggestively kinetic sense of hue that a gifted colourist can produce in a subtle composition. (Ada's hair is actually black; but Nabokov is aware of the way colours assume different values when orchestrated together and depending on the source of the light.) Thus, through individual, magically detailed imagination, Ada at the game-table, otherwise elusive as all objects of memory are elusive, is forced into the sensuous centre. What she means to the imagination of her enraptured beholder infinitely transcends the arithmetic scores of the anagrammatic game they have been playing; and the reference to past, present, and future is strategically important, because Ada as a luminous image treasured in the memory of the artist becomes an eternal present, beyond the ravages of time, is the fulfilled quest of the novel as a whole.

This evocation of Ada is not only artful but, like most of what happens in the novel, it is set against another artwork – the translucent lakescape of the parchment lampshade with its Japanese dragons. The most immediate function of this detail is to contribute to the scenic realization of the moment; but it is also, like so many other artworks that Nabokov introduces, an analogue and an inverted reflection of the world of the novel. The lampshade painting is executed, one assumes, with reticent Oriental brushstrokes quite unlike the Boschean descriptive vividness of the novel's technique. Instead of the serpents of Ada's Eden, there are Japanese dragons; instead of Ardis's rural streams, a lake. A more elaborate instance of Ada's being set off against serpentine art occurs earlier in the novel, when she is a still virginal, though already distinctly nubile, twelve-year-old:

> His sentimental education now went fast. Next morning, he happened to catch sight of her washing her face and arms over an old-fashioned basin on a rococo stand, her hair knotted on the top of her head, her nightgown twisted around her waist like a clumsy corolla out of which issued her slim back, rib-shaded on the near side. A fat snake of porcelain curled around the basin, and as both the reptile and he stopped to watch Eve and the soft woggle of her bud-breasts in profile, a big mulberry-colored cake of soap slithered out of her hand, and her black-socked foot hooked the door shut with a bang which was more the echo of the soap's crashing against the marble board than a sign of pudic displeasure.

As in the scene of Ada by the lamp, painterly attention is given to shading and colour, with that wonderful mulberry-coloured soap somehow bringing the whole scene into bright focus and, at the same time, introducing a delicate suggestion of gustatory delight into the vision of soapy Ada in her ritual of ablution. But, where Ada at the game-table was a static portrait, movement dominates this passage, from the scrubbing hands of the beginning through the soft woggle of the breasts in the middle to the door kicked shut at the end. Indeed, even what should logically be static begins strangely to move. Ada's slim back 'issues' from her pulled-down nightgown like an object in fluid motion; and the 'nightgown twisted' is a noun with a participle ambiguously turning itself into an active verb; so that the 'clumsy corolla' of the garment can provide a perfect compositional parallel, in floral imagery, to the fat porcelain snake curling around the basin. The snake's movement is then imparted to the bar of soap, which 'slithers' out of Ada's hand. The rococo serpent, of course, an item of aristocratic bric-à-brac, is permanently frozen as a piece of decorative sculpture, but seems to possess (or to have possessed) movement, it being in the nature of plastic art to create the illusion of kinesis out of perfect stasis. The enamoured Van, then, can wittily recruit the snake as a fellow-admirer of Ada's beauty, imagining that the reptile observer like himself has momentarily stopped in its tracks with amazement over what it beholds. A snake observing Eve obviously points back to that forever fateful moment at the beginning of Genesis; but this fat fellow seems more a jovial attendant to the young woman's loveliness than a sinister seductor. The question of where or whether evil enters the Veens' Eden, a place paradoxically rich in demonic nomenclature, is not easy to resolve; and we shall try to sort out some of the main elements of that issue in a moment.

First, however, I should like to point out how traditional this whole enterprise of realizing experience is, at least in one crucial respect. For the moments Van Veen recreates for us are not taken from indifferent topics. Almost all the truly memorable ones, like the three we have just considered, are sensuous meditations on the image of Ada. If he and she are two halves of a primal self, there is complementarity rather than equality between them, because he is the artist, she the subject, model, muse. Nabokov had at first thought of calling the novel *The Texture of Time*, a title he then relegated to a metaphysical work by Van Veen; but his book had to be called *Ada* for the same reason that the sundry sonnet-cycles of the English Renaissance were emblazoned with titles like *Delia*, *Diana*, *Phyllis*, *Celia*. Art, to borrow the vocabulary of the 'Viennese quack' Nabokov never tired of mocking, is a flow of libidinous energy towards the world, a formally coherent re-enactment – perhaps more intensification than compensation – of the pleasure the artist has known in the world. And for the male-dominated Western tradition, at least as far back as Dante, the emblem, talisman or goal of this pleasure is the figure of a beloved woman; it is through her that the artist comes to realize the fullness of life. 'He saw reflected in her', Van says of himself and Ada just before the end, 'everything that his fastidious and fierce spirit sought in life.'

Nabokov had played with this tradition once before in his other English novel bearing a woman's name as title; but *Lolita* is, of course, in many respects a highly ironic version of the myth of the Muse or Eternal Beloved, shrewdly raising all sorts of psychological and epistemological questions about what is involved in a man's addiction to such a myth. *Ada*, less novelistic and more lyric than its predecessor, attempts to renew the myth without ironic subversion, which may explain some of its weaknesses, but is also the reason for its distinctive beauty. At one point, Van is unsettled to learn that his love for Ada has become the subject among the inhabitants of the Ardis region of a whole cycle of romances, epics, folk songs, ballads sung to the strum of seven-stringed Russian lyres. His own task is to present a more scrupulous version that will not falsify the sensuous truth of his lifelong love, in a literary art that is in turn lyrical, painterly, wittily playful, scientific, aphoristic, self-reflective. The result of this effort will be the 'real' Ada, and a 589-page poem called *Ada*.

All this still leaves unexplained the lurking elements of shadow in Nabokov's large sunny picture. At several points in the novel the narrator takes pains to inform us that Ada is the genitive form of the Russian word for hell. This makes Ada an exact etymological antithesis of the Renaissance poet's fair beloved, Celia, a name formed from the Latin for heaven. The main point, I would assume, is that Ada and Van in their Eden are in a state before the knowledge of good and evil, when heaven and hell cannot be distinguished. This also suggests, however, that there could be an ambiguous underside of evil in the edenic fulfilment offered Van by his sister-soul; and the suicide to which the two of them inadvertently drive Lucette may indicate that a paradisiac love can have evil consequences when it impinges on the lives of others outside the Garden; that there may be something essentially destructive in a passion that is so relentlessly an *égotisme à deux*. An oddly grim fatality accompanies the long history of Ada's and Van's raptures. All four of their putative and actual parents come to a bad end, two of them being quite mad at the end, and one of them, Dan Veen, actually dying 'an odd Boschean death' under the delusion that he is being ridden by a huge rodent, a detail he remembers from Bosch's *The Garden of Earthly Delights*. Nabokov's invocation of that painting as one possible model for his own project in *Ada* is itself an indication that his notion of the representation of Eden had its darker aspects. Bosch is praised by Demon Veen for the sheer freedom of fantasy he exercised, 'just enjoying himself by crossbreeding casual fancies just for the fun of the contour and the colour, ... the exquisite surprise of an unusual orifice'; and presumably Nabokov means to emulate that uninhibited exuberance of invention in his novel. But *The Garden of Earthly Delights* is not merely, as Demon Veen contends, an expression of an artist's delight in freely manipulating the medium; it is also a disturbingly ambiguous conception of the terrestrial paradise. Its central panel, 'In Praise of Lust', is a panoramic representation of polymorphous perversity in which the actors look more often like doomed souls than gleeful sybarites. The right panel of the tryptitch, moreover, is no garden at all, but a vision of damnation against a black background, crowded with the usual Boschean monsters and eery images of dismemberment, and entitled, because of the huge musical instruments in the foreground, 'Musical Hell'.

Did Nabokov mean to suggest that there is something ultimately monstrous about the artistic imagination itself; that, given absolute freedom, it will conjure up not only beautiful birds of paradise but the most fearful monstrosities as well? (Here, as in other respects, there might be a moment of convergence between Nabokov's view of the mind and Freud's, however great the polemic distance that the novelist placed between himself and psychoanalysis.) Certainly Van Veen as the exemplary artist within the world of the novel gives one pause for thought. He may even be intended, as Ellen Pifer argues in a forthcoming book on the moral dimension of Nabokov's fiction, as another in the series of manipulative, sinister artist-figures that goes back to Axel Rex in *Laughter in the Dark*. There is something distinctly chilling about Van Veen's relation to everything and everyone except Ada and his own writing. Outside his private garden-world and his literary lucubrations, he is a snob, a cold sensualist, and even on occasion a violent brute (as when he blinds the blackmailer Kim by caning him across the eyes). But if it was Nabokov's intention somehow to expose Van Veen, it is an intention not held in steady focus; for it is clear that the author shares many aspects of Van's sensibility and imaginatively participates in Van's dearest artistic and metaphysical aspirations, inviting us as readers to do so as well. The perilous closeness of beauty and monstrosity is manifestly an idea Nabokov conjures with in this most ambitious, and most avowedly Boschean, of his novels; but it remains uncertain whether he actually succeeded in defining the relationship between those antitheses in fictionally cogent terms.

In any event, the ultimate sense that the novel means to project is of all threats of evil, including the evil of the corrosive passage of time, finally transcended by the twinned power of art and love. One last clue encodes this idea as a signature of affirmation at the end of the novel. Moving around mysteriously in the background of the concluding section is an unexplained figure named Ronald Oranger. Since he marries the typist responsible for Van's manuscript, and since he and his wife, according to a prefatory note, are the only significant persons mentioned in the book still alive when it is published, one may assume that his is the final responsibility for the text of *Ada*; and that he is the presiding spirit at the end. All we really know about him is his name, which, of course, means 'orange tree' in French. No orange trees are explicitly mentioned in Marvell's 'The Garden', though they are spectacularly present in 'Bermudas', another remarkable poem by Marvell about a garden-paradise. In any case, 'Ronald Oranger' in a Nabokov novel has a suspiciously anagrammatic look, and could well be rearranged as a reversal of the book's title, 'angel nor ardor' – which is to say, that the fixative force of art, working through the imagination of love, has extracted heaven from hell, Eden from Ada, has established a perfected state that originates in the carnal passions but goes quite beyond them.

Fortunately, the code-games and allusions in *Ada* are merely pointers to the peculiar nature of the novel's imaginative richness, which does not finally depend on the clues. Despite its incidental annoyances and even its occasional *longueurs*, few books written in our lifetime afford so much pleasure. Perhaps the parody-blurb at the end is not so wrong in proferring the novel as a voluminous bag of rare delights: Nabokov's garden abounds with the pleasurable visions whose artful design I have tried to sketch out here, and, as the blurb justifiably concludes, with 'much, much more'.

9 The Last Interview

Robert Robinson

We arrived in February. Wintry laurels and the bare willow trees made the path at the side of the lake seem melancholy, and there was a curious feeling of taking a walk in an old photograph. We were calling on Nabokov to let him know we were there, and also to tell him he'd given us rather short measure. The Nabokov interview (on this occasion for *The Book Programme* on BBC2) is an entirely structured affair: the questions are sent a fortnight or so before the event, the answers are composed and returned, and then all you have to do is get in front of a camera and *serve* the interview, like iced cake. But it was to be a twenty-five-minute programme, and he hadn't given us quite enough.

He had been very ill. When he came into one of the public rooms of that slightly left-over caravanserai, the Montreux Palace Hotel, he was leaning on a stick, his face was pale, and his collar was now a size or two too large. Mme Nabokov was with him and she, too, had been ill. I felt rather scared – I don't quite know why – and to my surprise, after we'd been talking for a few minutes and I'd said how agreeable it was to know the interview had already taken place, frozen on paper before the cameras arrived, precluding the possibility of anything unexpected, Mme Nabokov murmured in a low voice: 'Were you frightened?' I jumped up and cried, 'Oh no, not at all, not a bit,' but I suppose, in accepting the premise of so strange a question, I gave myself the lie.

As far as the length of the interview was concerned it was plain that Nabokov had said all that he wished to say, and wished to say no more. So it was decided that he would read one of his poems, and immediately, like a chef measuring out his ingredients in extraordinarily careful spoonfuls, he began to weigh the poem in terms of time: 'So many *strophes* at so many seconds a *strophe*, let us say fifteen *strophes*.' 'No, it is twelve,' interjected Mme Nabokov, 'twelve, then say thirty seconds for each *strophe*, multiplied by twelve – that gives us an extra six minutes – yes, it is quite enough.'

We weren't allowed into the Nabokov quarters – six rooms on the top floor of the hotel ('those *attics*', as Nabokov drily apostrophized them). We were excluded on the grounds of there not being space enough, but it would have been odd if a man who had devoted his life to holding the world entertainingly at bay should not have protected his privacy. So a faint social hiccup developed – we were calling on business, but they actually *lived* at the hotel – so that, when Nabokov said, 'We could go into the bar, if you wished to offer a drink', I thought he must have meant, 'if you wish to *be* offered a drink': but not only was this a slightly absurd indulgence to extend to a writer who always takes pains to say precisely what he wants to say, it just didn't quite feel as though the Nabokovs' were 'At Home'....

We drank some vodka ('Crepkaya, if it is for M. Nabokov,' the waiter murmured) and Nabokov explained that he would like some vodka on the table in front of him when the interview was filmed the following day – 'but because I do not wish to give a false impression and have people think I am an old drunk, let them put the vodka in a water-jug.' In short, he was saying that the illness had laid him low, and that the camera and the bright lights would tax his strength.

The next day a room at the Montreux Palace was lit for the cameras, and Nabokov seated himself at one of those Louis-the-Hotel tables, and propped his notes against the carafe that held the vodka, and we did the question and answer as I imagine Elizabethan actors conducted a duologue – moving stiffly through a sequence of conventional gestures and inflections which had been devised to relieve the participants of the idiocy of pretending the exchange was spontaneous. Neither Nabokov nor I made any attempt at *mime*: we lifted the cards to our eyes and read the words we had already exchanged on paper, aloud; at the end of the dance, I as it were handed my partner back to his seat and put on my glasses to read the words, 'Thank you, Mr Nabokov....'

Throughout the interview, Mme Nabokov had sat in a corner of the room, her hands clasped on her walking-stick, quite silent. I sensed her presence behind me throughout and, as I faced Nabokov, I felt her absorption too; he was all her care. The Nabokovs moved slowly out of the room, and I had some idea they were returning to a chess game they had left unfinished upstairs.

A blush of colour – Nabokov in Montreux

ROBERT ROBINSON: First, sir, to spare you irritation, I wonder if you will instruct me in the pronunciation of your name.

VLADIMIR NABOKOV: Let me put it this way. There exists a number of deceptively simple-looking Russian names, whose spelling and pronunciation present the foreigner with strange traps. The name Suvarov took a couple of centuries to lose the preposterous middle 'a' – it should be Suvoruv. American autograph-seekers, while professing a knowledge of all my books – prudently not mentioning their titles – rejuggle the vowels of my name in all the ways allowed by mathematics. 'Nabakav' is especially touching for the 'a's. Pronunciation problems fall into a less erratic pattern. On the playing-fields of Cambridge, my football team used to hail me as 'Nabkov' or facetiously, 'Macnab'. New Yorkers reveal their tendency of turning 'o' into 'ah' by pronouncing my name 'Nabarkov'. The aberration, 'N*a*bokov', is a favourite one of postal officials; now the correct Russian way would take too much time to explain, and so I've settled for the euphonious 'Nab*o*kov', with the middle syllable accented and rhyming with 'smoke'. Would you like to try?

RR: Mr NabOkov.

VN: That's right.

RR: You grant interviews on the understanding that they shall not be spontaneous. This admirable method ensures there will be no dull patches. Can you tell me why and when you decided upon it?

VN: I'm not a dull speaker, I'm a bad speaker, I'm a wretched speaker. The tape of my unprepared speech differs from my written prose as much as the worm differs from the perfect insect – or, as I once put it, I think like a genius, I write like a distinguished author and I speak like a child.

RR: You've been a writer all your life. Can you evoke for us the earliest stirring of the impulse?

VN: I was a boy of fifteen, the lilacs were in full bloom; I had read Pushkin and Keats; I was madly in love with a girl of my age, I had a new bicycle (an Enfield, I remember) with reversible handlebars that could turn it into a racer. My first poems were awful, but then I reversed those handlebars, and things improved. It took me, however, ten more years to realize that my true instrument was prose – poetic prose, in the special sense that it depended on comparisons and metaphors to say what it wanted to say. I spent the years 1925 to 1940 in Berlin, Paris, and the Riviera, after which I took off for America. I cannot complain of neglect on the part of any great critics, although as always and everywhere there was an odd rascal or two badgering me. What has amused me in recent years is that those old novels and stories published in English in the sixties and seventies, were appreciated much more warmly than they had been in Russian thirty years ago.

RR: Has your satisfaction in the act of writing ever fluctuated? I mean is it keener now or less keen than once it was?

VN: Keener.

RR: Why?

VN: Because the ice of experience now mingles with the fire of inspiration.

RR: Apart from the pleasure it brings, what do you conceive your task as a writer to be?

VN: This writer's task is the purely subjective one of reproducing as closely as possible the image of the book he has in his mind. The reader need not know, or, indeed, cannot know, what the image is, and so cannot tell how closely the book has conformed to its image in the author's mind. In other words, the reader has no business bothering about the author's intentions, nor has the author any business trying to learn whether the consumer likes what he consumes.

RR: Of course, the author works harder than the reader does; but I wonder whether it augments his – this is to say, your – pleasure that he makes the reader work hard, too.

VN: The author is pefectly indifferent to the capacity and condition of the reader's brain.

RR: Could you give us some idea of the pattern of your working day?

VN: This pattern has lately become blurry and inconstant. At the peak of the book, I worked all day, cursing the tricks that objects play upon me, the mislaid spectacles, the spilled wine. I also find talking of my working day far less entertaining than I formerly did.

RR: The conventional view of an hotel is as of a temporary shelter – one brings one's own luggage, after all – yet you choose to make it permanent.

VN: I have toyed on and off with the idea of buying a villa. I can imagine the comfortable furniture, the efficient burglar alarms, but I am unable to visualize an adequate staff. Old retainers require time to get old, and I wonder how much of it there still is at my disposal.

RR: You once entertained the possibility of returning to the United States. I wonder if you will.

VN: I will certainly return to the United States at the first opportunity. I'm indolent, I'm sluggish, but I'm sure I'll go back with tenderness. The thrill with which I think of certain trails in the Rockies is only matched by visions of my Russian woods, which I will never revisit.

RR: Is Switzerland a place with positive advantages for you, or is it simply a place without positive disadvantages?

VN: The winters can be pretty dismal here, and my old borzoi has developed feuds with lots of local dogs, but otherwise it's all right.

RR: You think and write in three languages – which would be the preferred one?

VN: Yes, I write in three languages, but I think in images. The matter of preference does not really arise. Images are mute, yet presently the silent cinema begins to talk and I recognize its language. During the second part of my life, it was generally English, my own brand of English – not the Cambridge variety, but still English.

RR: At any point do you invite your wife to comment on work in progress?

VN: When the book is quite finished, and its fair copy is still warm and wet, my wife goes carefully through it. Her comments are usually few but invariably to the point.

RR: Do you find that you re-read your own earlier work, and if you do, with what feelings?

VN: Re-reading my own works is a purely utilitarian business. I have to do it when correcting a paperback edition riddled with misprints or controlling a translation, but there are some rewards. In certain species – this is going to be a metaphor – in certain species, the wings of the pupated butterfly begin to show in exquisite miniature through the wing-cases of the chrysalis a few days before emergence. It is the pathetic sight of an iridescent future transpiring through the shell of the past, something of the kind I experience when dipping into my books written in the twenties. Suddenly through a drab photograph a blush of colour, an outline of form, seems to be distinguishable. I'm saying this with absolute scientific modesty, not with the smugness of ageing art.

RR: Which writers are you currently reading with pleasure?

VN: I'm re-reading Rimbaud, his marvellous verse and his pathetic correspondence in the Pléiade edition. I am also dipping into a collection of unbelievably stupid Soviet jokes.

RR: Your praise for Joyce and Wells has been high. Could you identify briefly the quality in each which sets them apart?

VN: Joyce's *Ulysses* is set apart from all modern literature, not only by the force of his genius, but also by the novelty of his form. Wells is a great writer, but there are many writers as great as he.

RR: Your distaste for the theories of Freud has sometimes sounded to me like the agony of one betrayed, as though the old magus had once fooled you with his famous three-card trick. Were you ever a fan?

VN: What a bizarre notion! Actually I always loathed the Viennese quack. I used to stalk him down dark alleys of thought, and now we shall never forget the sight of old, flustered Freud seeking to unlock his door with the point of his umbrella.

RR: The world knows that you are also a lepidopterist but may not know what that involves. In the collection of butterflies, could you describe the process from pursuit to display?

VN: Only common butterflies, showy moths from the tropics, are put on display in a dusty case between a primitive mask and a vulgar abstract picture. The rare, precious stuff is kept in the glazed drawers of museum cabinets. As for pursuit, it is, of course, ecstasy to follow an undescribed beauty, skimming over the rocks of its habitat, but it is also great fun to locate a new species among the broken insects in an old biscuit tin sent over by a sailor from some remote island.

RR: One can always induce a mild vertigo by recalling that Joyce might not have existed as the writer but as the tenor. Have you any sense of having narrowly missed some other role? What substitute could you endure?

VN: Oh, yes, I have always had a number of parts lined up in case the muse failed. A lepidopterist exploring famous jungles came first, then there was the chess grand master, then the tennis ace with an unreturnable service, then the goalie saving a historic shot, and finally, finally, the author of a pile of unknown writings – *Pale Fire*, *Lolita*, *Ada* – which my heirs discover and publish.

RR: Alberto Moravia told me of his conviction that each writer writes only of one thing – has but a single obsession he continually develops. Can you agree?

VN: I have not read Alberto Moravia but the pronouncement you quote is certainly wrong in my case. The circus tiger is not obsessed by his torturer, my characters cringe as I come near with my whip. I have seen a whole avenue of imagined trees losing their leaves at the threat of my passage. If I do have any obsessions I'm careful not to reveal them in fictional form.

RR: Mr Nabokov, thank you.

VN: You're welcome, as we say in my adopted country.

10 On Revisiting Father's Room

Dmitri Nabokov

'You have to have in you some cell, some gene, some germ that will vibrate in answer to sensations that you can neither define, nor dismiss. Beauty plus pity – that is the closest we can get to a definition of art. Where there is beauty there is pity, for the simple reason that beauty must die, beauty always dies; the manner dies with the matter, the world dies with the individual.'

Vladimir Nabokov, university lecture
on Kafka's *Metamorphosis*

Lake Geneva reflects, here and there, the last details of a sunset, the mirrory surface broken only by a semicircular ripple of wake that the aged evening sidewheeler leaves as it rounds the point of Clarens on its way to Lausanne and Geneva. Pinkish contrails criss-cross the sky, like a grid for some gigantic game of tic-tac-toe. The top of the ancient lakeside pine, where a large crow takes its midday break, is now vacant.

On the far, French, side of Lake Léman stands a minor mountain group, foothill to the Mont Blanc massif. Seen from our Montreux windows it is a classic triple formation: two ancillary summits, whose slopes drop into the lake, flanking a little suspended valley that leads inland to the central, highest pyramid. These are not the professional peaks, with their moraines, icefalls, and precipitous rock faces, that both Father and I knew well, but a friendly little group, whose topographic and aesthetic harmony lures the viewer's eye into its depths. Often my parents and I would look into that miniature magic world and plan to take the tempting road that switchbacks up the left sub-peak and curls into the meadows and hamlets of the alpine valley beyond, to sample the panorama at close quarters at last, to see what butterflies were available, and to look back on Montreux from those slopes. Father, who so much yearned to make that outing, was invariably sidetracked by other matters while in Montreux; and, when time would come for summer travels, distant hotel-rooms would be reserved, cars loaded, and little fairytale Grammont would be left for another month or year. The longer we postponed this simple pleasure, the more mysterious and inaccessible it grew. We never did go; and it was, in a sense, a joy, I think for Father as well as for me, to let that toy mountain world live on, unspoiled and full of hidden pleasures, preserved as each of us, in his mind's eye, wished to see it.

After sunset in September it grows suddenly cooler in Montreux. It is time to close the window and withdraw my thoughts into the room. Now, when in Montreux, I sleep here; but for years it was Father's little lair, where he would write, read, and rest, and from which he would emerge, during periods of intense creative concentration, only for a hurried, absent-minded meal, or to share some amusing tidbit with Mother and with me. The room still retains many of the touches only Father could impart. For example, the huge old wooden floor-lamp with its enormous shade on which the practised eye can distinguish a splendidly detailed butterfly here, hidden as in a Flemish still-life, or a funny little chap there, worked into and around the garland design and its yellowed background, traversed by myriad small cracks. The furniture is rearranged now; and that marvellous lectern at which he would begin his writing day is gone. But here, propped against the desk's rear parapet, is the unframed, faded, and dusty reproduction of Fra Beato Angelico's *L'Annunciazione*, brought from Italy by Aunt Elena, with the rigid angel making his announcement on one knee. And, pencilled underneath in Father's minute, meticulous hand, referring to the angel's stylized rainbow wings: 'A recollection of *Iphiclides podalirius* with a slight dash of *Papilio machaon* and perhaps a hint of the day-flying moth *Panaxia quadripunctaria*. The two blackish stripes of each "wing" correspond to the pattern of *I. podalirius* in the natural position of rest' – then an asterisk joined by a line to another in the vertical margin – 'see Portmann, *Animal Forms*, p. 110, NY 1967'.

For years he had longed to do that never-to-be book on butterflies in art. Discovering a perfect *Vanessa atalanta* concealed in a Brueghel bush thrilled him almost as much as spotting a rare mutant on the wing.

There are, in the rooms, shelves of art books – loved by Mother, used by Father in his search – and butterfly books, and a rich variety of reference works. Here is an American dictionary with the national eagle on its olive-brown cover transformed into a magnificent furry hawk moth. Ornithological and botanical texts too, for he took pride in identifying every plant and bird encountered. How he lectured me, on a lakeside walk, for confusing a linden with an elm! What joy all three of us took in observing the grebes and coots on the lake, and the graceful, yellow-beaked alpine choughs that often perched on our balcony.

Father loved both the bird and the word. It delighted him that three species of owl – the common scops and long-eared owls, and the rarer eagle owl – are known in French as *petit-duc*, *moyen-duc*, and *grand-duc*. The two larger duke owls, in fact, made a quick appearance in 'A Visit to the Museum'. Often, pencilled into the bird books, is the exact Russian name, and one of them is Sirin (for his Russian *nom de plume* of the twenties and thirties was that of the hawk owl as well as of the fabled bird).

It was in this room that I found Father on my return from a trip to the United States in the late winter of 1977. He had been discharged from the hospital, thin and weak but declared clinically cured. We began once again going for walks – not the alpine rambles of previous years, but a few hundred feet, up and down the Grand-Rue. Father always had a cheerful quip for the druggist and news-vendor, and never once complained of his weakness. His courage, his love of life, and his trusting, gentle nature were to remain with him to the end. If there is a quality overlooked in his writing by some of the more obtuse commentators, it is that gentleness, coupled with a total honesty on every plane and an utter freedom from anything cruel, cheap, or mean. I recall his pang of pity upon seeing the grisly newsreels at the time of John Kennedy's assassination – not only for the dead president, but also for a still innocent (inasmuch as only suspected) Oswald, shown bruised and black-eyed: 'If they have worked over (*zamoochili*) this poor little guy (*chelovechka*) needlessly . . . ,' he said, with the menacing tone he used only when defending the weak and blameless, whether animal or human. When the facts were established his attitude obviously changed. But I wonder how many people had such a first reaction.

If Father had a defect, it was an openness to and trust of others, a goodness bordering sometimes on ingenuousness, an instinctive assumption that others were as good as he until proven otherwise. Else he might never have let certain scoundrels come close. How funny – and how wretched – the grudging concession of a recent biographer: 'He is, I reckon, a good man, oh, in a peculiar way perhaps, and with certain lapses, but a good man none the less.'

However, to paraphrase Chateaubriand, let me not narrow the field of my contempt to one recipient, when others, too, are needy. The embittered would-be Pushkinist, for instance, who rears up to launch a posthumous assault on Father's translation of, and commentary to, *Eugene Onegin.* The man's credentials, though, are not totally convincing, and his objectivity might be more persuasive if he were not the perpetrator of a versified version of the same work, withdrawn by its publisher, to be replaced by an only slightly improved edition after Father had pointed out some of the most blatant howlers.

I shall, however, follow Father's example and not pursue polemics with the unworthy. It is far better to let lying dogs sleep, and instead pay attention to those blessed with the gift (for a gift it is) of tuning in on the poetic genius and the profound humanity of the utterly original Nabokov, and with the dignity to criticize, if they so choose, not out of ignorance or Salierian envy, but with dispassionate conviction.

On those late-winter walks I was somehow sure that Father's once powerful body would recover its strength, that I would see him once again fit and tanned, in shorts and climbing shoes on an Alpine slope, butterfly net in hand and a novel working in his mind. The last time we had had a good tramp together in the mountains had been at Rougemont, near Gstaad, a couple of summers before. He told me then, in one of those rare moments when father and son discuss such matters, that he had accomplished what he wished in life and art, and was a truly happy man. His writing, he went on, was all there, ready inside his mind, like film waiting to be developed. A sensation, he said, akin to Schopenhauer's vision of events as they unfold.

Yet there was other film, still to be developed – words to be pencilled on those virgin, one-sided, made-to-order Bristol cards that I find in his old room. There are boxes of notes, too, for the butterflies-in-painting book, and sketches of lepidoptera organs for scientific studies. (How odd, by the way, that some fool, unable to comprehend that a *violon d'Ingres* can have multiple strings, has not attributed Father's concentration on the genitalia as a method for identifying subordinate forms to a prurient interest in the butterfly as nymphet! Or perhaps some fool has.) And there is another, very special box, containing a substantial part of the breathtakingly original *Original of Laura*, which would have been Father's most brilliant novel, the most concentrated distillation of his creativity, but whose release in incomplete form he expressly forbade.

It saddens me greatly that these works will remain incomplete and unpublished, but simultaneously it is a source of joy that other material will appear, thanks to devoted Nabokovians like Carl Proffer, whose *Ardis* has reissued many of Father's works in the original Russian, has published the author's Russian translations of *Lolita* and *Speak, Memory*, and is about to put out a good, thick volume of Nabokov's Russian verse, perhaps the most innovative, most tender, and most haunting of all his work.

Although adamant in his conviction that his energies must be channelled into creation, rather than into dialogue with critics, aspiring writers, or sundry correspondents, the response of certain people touched him deeply: the Proffers, the Appels, the Parkers; the special fine-tuned, A-plus readers; those fans who pointedly omitted not only the usual autograph card, but even a return address, and who were to sign their condolence telegrams 'a devoted reader' or 'a little Nabokov'. It is to them that the specialized Nabokoviana is addressed: the beautiful recording, by Spoken Arts, of Father reading from his English verse and from *Lolita*; the Cornell lectures that will soon be published; the stories and plays still to be translated.

In a world of establishment and jet-set writers, of bookstore autograph orgies and cut-throat battles for this or that literary award, it is a tribute of sorts to Nabokov's utter disdain for publicity that, upon his death, many newspapers, looking no further than a haywire wire service, printed the wrong photograph (that of his cousin Nicholas, who was to die less than a year later), some even calling Vladimir Nabokov a 'Soviet' writer. Or that a reportorial obituary channel, again with echoes far and wide, as if totally incredulous of what Father had actually said (that he could not care less), ascribed to him an expression of chagrin – evidently considered *de rigueur* among your garden-variety literary mafia – at never having won the Swedish prize. Particularly amusing were the well-meaning Italian television commemoration, a year after his death, that bestowed on him three wives and a proto-nymphet daughter (this, of course, came *in toto* from his last novel, *Look at the Harlequins*, via a tongue-in-cheek magazine interview consulted by some pony-tailed research assistant); and the society columnist for a French women's weekly, who proudly announced that he had encountered *Lolita*'s (presumably resurrected and rejuvenated) author – rather than the author's son – at a Geneva party well into 1978.

In some circles Nabokov's fame still consists of the miscomprehensions that arose from his famous – or notorious – *Lolita* ... Other readers take him to be a morbid sensualist, a chess-obsessed player of verbal games, a trickster out to baffle his readers.... The cure, if one is conceivable, lies not in explaining each of Nabokov's novels, in detail, to each of his readers, but rather in explaining to them the contents and workings of Nabokov's individual and specific mind.*

Thus writes J. D. O'Hara, who understands well Father's conviction that the individual and his art are sacrosanct, unique and unclassifiable, and not to be violated by political tyranny, by Freudian generalization, by schools, movements, and categories, or by approximate translation that reads well.

How misunderstood was poor Lolita! What a pornocopia of pubescent and post-pubescent prostitutes has travelled through the media under her name! And when the pathetic lady at a cocktail party, in her cups, inquires with a conspiratorial smirk, 'How does it feel to have a dirty old man for a father?', what can one answer? That she is in the same league with those purchasers who took only the second volume of the original two-tome *Lolita*, because it was supposedly more scabrous? That foul language does not exist in Father's books? That every sentence he wrote was poetry, and poetry cannot be dirty? That a creative genius does not have to experience the madness of his various characters to give them life? That he was the most totally honourable individual I have ever met? That every word of his possessed a twinkle of humour, and that everything – even the most ordinary household announcement or *pro memoria* to himself, to Mother, or to me – had an extraordinary, original and endearing twist? 'How often did I enviously say to myself, "I wish I had been capable of putting it that way!"'

I treasure his little notes to me, such as the one that accompanied the proof of *Look at the Harlequins*, given to me for a pre-publication glance (again I transliterate the Russian):

[added at top of card, in view of my arrival]
You can use my toilet remains
and *nochnye toofli* [slippers]!

June 4, 1974

(Auction price of this card *circa* 2000 AD at least 5000 roubles.)

Dmitrichko [a diminutive not used before or since]!

Here is a copy of LATH 'acronym' for you to read carefully and lovingly.

* J. D. O'Hara, 'Reading Nabokov', in *Canto*, Spring 1977.

Vladimir Nabokov

Main queries: technical or idiomatic slips. Mark your queries or corrections with birdies in margin and explain them on a page of the notebook (with butterflies) provided by the author.

Easy on spelling and punctuation: there are editors for that.

... words unfamiliar (or objectionable) to you ... are likely to be in my large Webster or 13-vols OED, or else are noncewords (from 'once' not from 'nonsense') of my make.

Loving regards
VN

And when that butterfly-bedecked notebook, marked 'for Dmitri's notes', was later returned to me like a corrected examination pamphlet, it contained, among the routine marginal notes in answer to my comments ('yes', 'no', 'it's OK', *'ikh delo'* [their problem]), the following little gems:

[to my question as to why Father insisted on inserting certain commas for clarity where I, something of a pedant in these matters, claimed they should not go]
I like privacy.

[regarding a typo that deprived 'Leningrad' of an 'n' for the fourth or fifth time]
cette pauvre ville!

[in Russian, when I erred in the final digit of a page number]
We're getting a wee bit tired, and understandably so.

[in Russian, next to a couple of pinkish blots from a cut finger or from wine on a moving train]
What is this? And this?

In some small measure, I learned from Father to collect the kind of special observations and fleeting thoughts we used to share occasionally. He had a rich supply of them, carded away for future use, like unspread butterflies in opaque envelopes. When a new item clicks into my consciousness, my first mental reflex is the thought of bringing it to Father for approval, like a sea-levitated stone on a Riviera beach in childhood; and only a split-pang later do I realize there is no Father. Would he have liked my little offerings? The Roman *piazza*, called Margana, which yields, read backwards, 'anagram'. The inscription 'Ball Trap', glimpsed on a roadside poster on the Grande Corniche: Franglais for some village game, or disco nomenclature at a new low? The elderly green London removal van I saw in Juan-les-Pins the other day, emblazoned

'Tooth Transport' (does it travel one way loaded with discarded molars, to return with a cargo of glistening bridges and crowns? Had the name 'Tooth Removals' been considered and rejected?). The stateside tourist on the Carlton Terrace, during the Cannes Film Festival, holding up a miniature poodle for a look at Cassius Clay, present for some promotion stunt or other, presumably so that the innocent little dog might one day tell its children and grandchildren. In a café, the rapid movement of two heads, as menus are distributed: the myopic forward, the presbyopic back. The photograph, in the local Vaud newspaper, of a Swiss mountain called Dent-Favre, unwitting monument to our Boston dentist of thirty years ago, a Swiss named Dr Favre. A massive, reddish First World War memorial in a town near Genoa, a monstrosity like most statuary *à clef*, with a sphinx-like centrepiece that a quick double-take reveals to be a matching, motionless, real reddish cat. Annie Sexi and the Johann Strauss Motorboat Works in the Vienna telephone book. The passing thought that, in search of a *mot juste* or rhyme, one sometimes sifts through the alphabet in desperation as if rapidly spinning the tuning knob of a radio: distant signals come in here and there; then, if in luck, you zero in.

Or the things seen from a fast-moving train to Zurich: bits of spring and early-summer landscape – rural roads that begin with a fairly respectable asphalt coating, gradually degenerate into a pair of earthy ruts, and peter out in a pasture (though sometimes they go through an exciting reverse process and, just when all hope for them has been abandoned, mature once again to full-fledged blacktop status); tracks that whip away on a tangent to hurry to some minor town; rusty rails, doomed from the start, that dwindle amid unkempt undergrowth. A trackside orchard casting a sun-dappled geometric pattern on the ground. What childhood memories of railway trips and country sojourns are evoked by the rural landscape, with all that the word 'rural', or, better yet, its Russian equivalent *derevenskoye*, connotes to me (who, by choice, have never been to Russia): fields of grain, sudden patches of wild weed inside a copse, spirals of cow dung, a dirt road with a succession of puddles and damp patches over which blue butterflies must hover. Why is it all so different, so heart-rendingly poetic, when isolated by the windows of a speeding summer train? Why is its poignancy so strongly amplified by the anguish of a family tragedy?

Or the farcical, posthumous juxtaposition, straight out of

Nabokov: a funeral director with assistant, playing their roles to the hilt, seated at our dining-room table to discuss various pointless details as long-haired young technicians bustle past them with a hired television (the black-and-white mistakenly delivered and rejected, the colour tested at length and at loud volume on sporting events and kids' shows) so that Mother and I may see the obituaries on the evening news.

March of 1977 was unseasonably warm. At mid-month I went to Geneva to hear a friend in *The Marriage of Figaro*. One experiences a tingle of excitement at the thought of going out coatless after months of dreary cold, to sample the first foretaste of spring. But the weather changed abruptly, and, when I came out of the hot Grand Théâtre at midnight, I was met by gusts of chilly wind. The next evening I had a dry cough which it became increasingly difficult to attribute to a passing irritation or the insufficiently humidified hotel air. The following day I was in bed with a respectable fever, and Mother, too, was coming down with the bug. Although I had begged my parents not to come close, that evening my gentle father padded into my room with a trayful of food and a volume of de Musset for me to read. A couple of days later his voice grew husky, and he started clearing his throat more often than usual; but for several days he insisted he was fine.

Soon, however, he was bedridden with a climbing temperature. Then it was the ambulance again, the Lausanne hospital with its doctors (who again announced that they had finally isolated the germ), the prospect of discharge in a few days, and the relapses, and Father's kind, still hopeful eyes, when he told me he was proud of me as I left for my Munich opera début.

Those first summery days in Munich were happier for me than any that were to follow: though ill, Father still existed. The city's periphery still retains a bit of country flavour, and, with its brand-new greenery and its evocative childhood smells, it gave a sensation of bustling spring well-being. Returning, from one of my long walks, towards a more populated area, along a paved path between some neat *Kleingartens* on the right and a mélange of older and more recent buildings on the left, I suddenly saw a brief stretch of railway track that sprang mysteriously out of a leafy grove to end, just as abruptly, a short distance away near a ramshackle structure that had once been some kind of workshop. Particularly in childhood, but later as well, I had been sensitive to the romance and mystery of trains (a sensitivity perhaps acquired or inherited from Father, through whose poetry and prose sleek steam locomotives and veneer-sided *wagons-lits* hauntingly travel). I felt an echo of the strange childhood excitement I used to experience when, during rambles through the woods in the South of France, I would hope against hope that certain horizontal formations of roots along a tree-shaded path would magically evolve, a little further on, into steel rails. In a sense, after so many years, the Munich tracks, just as mysterious, unrailwaylike, and part of the natural furnishings as had been those childhood roots, offered, at last, a fulfilment of the fantasy. What a thrill it would have been, as a boy, to conjecture whether a train would ever pass over them again!

How odd that this trip to Munich, during the last weeks of Father's life, should have been so rich in Nabokovian happenings. Strangest of all was my experience at Linderhof, the smallest and most private of mad Ludwig's castles. Having little of the local language, I joined a squad of tourists led by an English-speaking guide, leaving the Munich girl I had come with in a German-language contingent close on our heels. On my way through the little ornate rooms I paused to take a picture, and, when I detached my eye from the camera, found myself amid a totally different group. Thinking for a moment it was the one my friend had joined, I started searching for her face in the close-packed crowd. As I uneasily moved to and fro, I noticed an odd thing: the tourists and their guide seemed to look through me, as if I were not there. Mara had vanished; the gilded peacocks before me seemed eerily familiar; and I had the panicky feeling of being trapped in a cycle, doomed for ever to tour those rooms. Finding some stairs, I fought my way down through another and yet another wave of climbing visitors and, at last, miraculously, ran into my original guide, who, with a strange, knowing smile, ushered me through an unexpected door into a hidden passage that must once have been part of the servants' quarters. Suddenly I was quite alone. At the end of the passage was a second door. I opened it and emerged into what I half expected to be another time or land, so akin were those weird wanderings to the nightmarish atmosphere of a story of Father's, in which the exit from a provincial French museum gives on the wintry landscape of a forbidden Russia.

These two extraordinary Munich days are indelibly imprinted with the memory of Father: not only did they seem part of Father's personal world, where reality had an ever-present halo of poetic fantasy and childhood recollection; but they were the last impressions that I was to share with him.

He was home again when I returned to Montreux in June, but not well. Soon the fever mounted once again. His attitude, in those final days, was one of resignation; but now and then one had an inkling of how deeply hurt he felt at the thought of being suddenly cut off, because of a banal but dangerous trifle, from a life whose every detail gave him joy, and from a creative process in its fullest swing. Soon he went back to the Lausanne Hospital complex, where one entrance sign announced no parking for anyone except '*pompes funèbres et porteurs de macarons*' (funeral pumps and macaroon-bearers?), and the horrid hospital paraphernalia accumulated in his room in ever greater bulk.

As Mother and I waited for the professors' pregnant pauses to give birth, the air of condescending reassurance had disappeared, and one had the troubling sensation that the physicians' manner was changing from bedside to graveside. The end was quick: a chance draft from door and window simultaneously left open by an incautious, sneezing maid. Bronchial congestion suddenly more severe. The powerful heart that had endured strain after strain stilled with an abrupt threefold moan; the mind that loved life to the last, extinguished. Mother and I knew he was conscious, simply too weak to react, until the very end, not 'feeling nothing' as the doctors would have preferred us to believe. So perhaps our being present helped a little.

A few days before he died there was a moment I remember with special clarity. During our penultimate farewell, after I had kissed his still-warm forehead – as I had for years when saying goodnight or goodbye – tears suddenly welled in Father's eyes. I asked him why. He replied that a certain butterfly was already on the wing; and his eyes told me he no longer hoped that he would live to pursue it again. Nor would he ever visit that enchanted mountain valley on the far side of the lake. But perhaps, in Father's memory, I shall.

Bibliography of Nabokov's Major Works

Novels

CAMERA OBSCURA, translated by Winifred Roy, John Long, London, 1936. New edition translated by the author, with the title LAUGHTER IN THE DARK, Bobbs-Merrill, Indianapolis and New York, 1938; new edition, New Directions, New York, 1960; Weidenfeld, London, 1961.

DESPAIR, translated by the author, John Long, London, 1937; Putnam, New York, 1966; Weidenfeld, London, 1966.

THE REAL LIFE OF SEBASTIAN KNIGHT, New Directions, Norfolk, Conn., 1941; Edition Poetry, London, 1945.

BEND SINISTER, Henry Holt, New York, 1947; Weidenfeld, London, 1960.

LOLITA (in 2 volumes) Olympia Press, Paris, 1955; (one volume) Putnam, New York, 1958; Weidenfeld, London, 1959.

PNIN, Doubleday, New York, 1957; Heinemann, London, 1957.

INVITATION TO A BEHEADING, translated by Dmitri Nabokov in collaboration with the author. Putnam, New York, 1959; Weidenfeld, London, 1960.

PALE FIRE, Putnam, New York, 1962; Weidenfeld, London, 1962.

THE GIFT, translated by Michael Scammell with the collaboration of Dmitri Nabokov and the author, Putnam, New York, 1963; Weidenfeld, London, 1963.

THE DEFENCE (THE DEFENSE), translated by Michael Scammell in collaboration with the author, Putnam, New York, 1964; Weidenfeld, London, 1964.

THE EYE, translated by Dmitri Nabokov in collaboration with the author, Phaedra, New York, 1965; Weidenfeld, London, 1966.

KING, QUEEN, KNAVE, translated by Dmitri Nabokov in collaboration with the author, McGraw-Hill, New York, 1968; Weidenfeld, London, 1968.

ADA, OR ARDOR: A FAMILY CHRONICLE, McGraw-Hill, New York, 1969; Weidenfeld, London, 1969.

MARY, translated by Michael Glenny in collaboration with the author, McGraw-Hill, New York, 1970; Weidenfeld, London, 1971.

GLORY, translated by Dmitri Nabokov in collaboration with the author, McGraw-Hill, New York, 1972; Weidenfeld, London, 1972.

TRANSPARENT THINGS, McGraw-Hill, New York, 1972; Weidenfeld, London, 1973.

Vladimir Nabokov

LOOK AT THE HARLEQUINS!, McGraw-Hill, New York, 1974; Weidenfeld, London, 1975.

Collections

NINE STORIES ('The Aurelian', 'Cloud, Castle, Lake', 'Spring in Fialta', 'Mademoiselle O', 'A Forgotten Poet', 'The Assistant Producer', 'That in Aleppo Once ...', 'Time and Ebb', 'Double Talk'), New Directions, Norfolk, Conn., 1947.

NABOKOV'S DOZEN: *thirteen stories* (includes NINE STORIES but 'Conversation Piece, 1945' is new title for 'Double Talk', 'First Love', 'Signs and Symbols', 'Scenes from the Life of a Double Monster', 'Lance'), Doubleday, New York, 1958; Heinemann, London, 1959.

NABOKOV'S QUARTET ('An Affair of Honour', 'Lik', 'The Visit to the Museum', translated by Dmitri Nabokov; 'The Vane Sisters', written in English), Phaedra, New York, 1966; Weidenfeld, London, 1967.

A RUSSIAN BEAUTY AND OTHER STORIES, translated by Dmitri Nabokov and Simon Karlinsky in collaboration with the author, McGraw-Hill, New York, 1973; Weidenfeld, London, 1973.

STRONG OPINIONS, collection of interviews, letters to editors, and articles, McGraw-Hill, New York, 1973; Weidenfeld, London, 1974.

TYRANTS DESTROYED, AND OTHER STORIES, McGraw-Hill, New York, 1975; Weidenfeld, London, 1975.

DETAILS OF A SUNSET AND OTHER STORIES, McGraw-Hill, New York, 1976; Weidenfeld, London, 1976.

Poetry

POEMS, (with drawings by Robin Jacques), Doubleday, New York, 1959; Weidenfeld, London, 1961.

POEMS AND PROBLEMS, poems in Russian with English version by the author, poems written in English, and a series of chess problems, McGraw-Hill, New York, 1970; Weidenfeld, London, 1972.

Memoirs

CONCLUSIVE EVIDENCE: *A Memoir*, Harper Bros., New York, 1951. This was published in England as *Speak, Memory: A Memoir*, Gollancz, 1951. A revised edition with the title *Speak, Memory: An Autobiography Revisited* was published by Putnam, New York, 1967; Weidenfeld, London, 1966.

Literary Criticism

NIKOLAI GOGOL, Makers of Modern Literature series, New Directions, Norfolk, Conn., 1944; Edition Poetry, London, 1947; Weidenfeld, London, 1973.

Translations

PUSHKIN, LERMONTOV, TYUTCHEV: POEMS, Lindsay Drummond, London, 1947; Transatlantic Arts, New York, 1949.

HERO OF OUR TIME by Mikhail Lermontov, translated in collaboration with Dmitri Nabokov, Doubleday, New York, 1958.

THE SONG OF IGOR'S CAMPAIGN: *An Epic of the 12th Century*, translated from Old Russian, Random House, New York, 1960; Weidenfeld, London, 1961.

EUGENE ONEGIN: *A Novel in Verse* by Alexander S. Pushkin, translated, with a commentary, in 4 volumes: Vol. 1 Translator's introduction; Eugene Onegin; Vols 2 and 3 Commentary, appendix; Vol. 4 Index, photographic reproduction of the 1837 edition; Pantheon, New York, 1964; Routledge & Kegan Paul, London, 1954; revised edition with Russian/English parallel text, Routledge, 1976.